Legalir...

Editorial Advisors:
Gloria A. Aluise
  Attorney at Law
Jonathan Neville
  Attorney at Law
Robert A. Wyler
  Attorney at Law

Authors:
Gloria A. Aluise
  Attorney at Law
Daniel O. Bernstine
  Attorney at Law
Roy L. Brooks
  Professor of Law
Scott M. Burbank
  C.P.A.
Charles N. Carnes
  Professor of Law
Paul S. Dempsey
  Professor of Law
Jerome A. Hoffman
  Professor of Law
Mark R. Lee
  Professor of Law
Jonathan Neville
  Attorney at Law
Laurence C. Nolan
  Professor of Law
Arpiar Saunders
  Attorney at Law
Robert A. Wyler
  Attorney at Law

CONTRACTS

Adaptable to Sixth Edition*
of Knapp Casebook

By Jonathan Neville
Attorney at Law

*If your casebook is a newer edition, go to www.gilbertlaw.com
to see if a supplement is available for this title.

THOMSON
WEST

EDITORIAL OFFICE: 1 N. Dearborn Street, Suite 650, Chicago, IL 60602
REGIONAL OFFICES: Chicago, Dallas, Los Angeles, New York, Washington, D.C.

SERIES EDITOR
Linda C. Schneider, J.D.
Attorney at Law

PRODUCTION MANAGER
Elizabeth G. Duke

FIRST PRINTING—2009

Legalines®

**Features Detailed Briefs of Every Major Case,
Plus Summaries of the Black Letter Law**

Titles Available

Administrative Law .... Keyed to Breyer	Criminal Law .... Keyed to Dressler
Administrative Law .... Keyed to Schwartz	Criminal Law .... Keyed to Johnson
Administrative Law .... Keyed to Strauss	Criminal Law .... Keyed to Kadish
Antitrust .... Keyed to Areeda	Criminal Law .... Keyed to Kaplan
Antitrust .... Keyed to Pitofsky	Criminal Law .... Keyed to LaFave
Business Associations .... Keyed to Klein	Criminal Procedure .... Keyed to Kamisar
Civil Procedure .... Keyed to Friedenthal	Domestic Relations .... Keyed to Wadlington
Civil Procedure .... Keyed to Hazard	Estates and Trusts .... Keyed to Dobris
Civil Procedure .... Keyed to Yeazell	Evidence .... Keyed to Mueller
Conflict of Laws .... Keyed to Currie	Evidence .... Keyed to Waltz
Constitutional Law .... Keyed to Brest	Family Law .... Keyed to Areen
Constitutional Law .... Keyed to Choper	Income Tax .... Keyed to Freeland
Constitutional Law .... Keyed to Cohen	Income Tax .... Keyed to Klein
Constitutional Law .... Keyed to Rotunda	Labor Law .... Keyed to Cox
Constitutional Law .... Keyed to Stone	Property .... Keyed to Cribbet
Constitutional Law .... Keyed to Sullivan	Property .... Keyed to Dukeminier
Contracts .... Keyed to Calamari	Property .... Keyed to Nelson
Contracts .... Keyed to Dawson	Property .... Keyed to Rabin
Contracts .... Keyed to Farnsworth	Remedies .... Keyed to Rendelman
Contracts .... Keyed to Fuller	Securities Regulation .... Keyed to Coffee
Contracts .... Keyed to Kessler	Torts .... Keyed to Dobbs
Contracts .... Keyed to Knapp	Torts .... Keyed to Epstein
Contracts .... Keyed to Murphy	Torts .... Keyed to Franklin
Corporations .... Keyed to Choper	Torts .... Keyed to Henderson
Corporations .... Keyed to Eisenberg	Torts .... Keyed to Prosser
Corporations .... Keyed to Hamilton	Wills, Trusts & Estates .... Keyed to Dukeminier

All Titles Available at Your Law School Bookstore

THOMSON
™
WEST

SHORT SUMMARY OF CONTENTS

TABLE OF CONTENTS AND SHORT REVIEW OUTLINE

I. AN INTRODUCTION TO THE STUDY OF CONTRACT LAW

A. INTERPRETATION AND ENFORCEMENT OF PROMISES

1. **General Description.** The law of contracts deals with the interpretation and enforcement of promises. The performance of promises is one of the foundations of a civilized society, and enforcement of private contracts is a major function of the legal system. Integral to enforcement is interpretation of the words chosen by the contracting parties; hence, much of contract law involves rules for interpretation. Because the legislatures that create the rules and the courts that apply them are public institutions, contract law reflects prevailing cultural value systems.

2. **Lawyer's Role.** In contract law, a lawyer participates in the initial formation of a client's position, the negotiation with the other party, the drafting of the agreement, and the litigation of contract disputes. Success in each of these roles requires a thorough understanding of the terminology and principles behind contract law.

3. **Basic Terms.** Among the many terms used in contract law, the following are some of the most basic.

   a. **Promise.** A "promise" is an assurance that one will do or refrain from doing a specified thing. The Restatement (Second) requires the manifestation of intent to be made so as to justify the other party in understanding that a commitment has been made as to what will or will not be done in the future. Promises enforceable by law are called contracts.

   b. **Promisor.** The "promisor" is the person who makes the promise.

   c. **Promisee.** The person to whom the promise is addressed is called the "promisee."

   d. **Beneficiary.** When performance of a promise will benefit someone other than the promisee, that person is called the "beneficiary."

   e. **Consideration.** "Consideration" is a benefit received by the promisor or a detriment incurred by the promisee.

B. THE SOURCES OF CONTRACT LAW

1. **Judicial Opinions.** Like other common law, contract law developed as judge-made law. The law of contracts as developed through case law is fluid; it

reflects the tensions between (i) individual freedom to negotiate terms and enter binding contracts, and (ii) the public interest in various types of social control. Even though many of the cases studied are very old, the problems they raise recur regularly in our day.

2. **Statutory Law.** Until the 1940s, most contract law was derived from case law. The principal exception is the Statute of Frauds, which the English Parliament enacted in 1677 and is still almost universally observed. The Uniform Commercial Code ("U.C.C.") is a model code adopted in one form or another by all the states. The provisions most relevant to a basic course in contracts are contained in Article 2 (Sales), which applies to transactions in goods.

3. **The Restatements.** The first Restatement was published in 1932 by the American Law Institute. The Restatement (Second) refines and updates the first and correlates with the U.C.C. The Restatements are not statutory law; they are simply attempts to restate the common law of cases in a rule-like form. Although not binding on the courts, they are persuasive authority. Legal commentaries such as those contained in law reviews and treatises are also influential.

4. **International Law.** International transactions may present choice of law issues beyond the scope of this outline. An international body has drafted a type of international Restatement to help guide parties and courts: the UNIDROIT Principles of International Commercial Contracts. It is not legally binding, however. The Convention for the International Sale of Goods ("CISG") is an international treaty that acts as a code similar to the U.C.C. It is binding on domiciliaries of signatory nations, including the United States, unless the parties provide otherwise in their contract. It only applies to international contracts.

C. TYPES OF CONTRACTS

Courts recognize three types of contractual arrangements: (i) express contracts; (ii) implied-in-fact contracts; and (iii) implied-in-law contracts, or quasi-contracts.

1. **Express Contracts.** An express contract may be oral or written. It consists of an offer, acceptance, and bargained-for consideration. It may be bilateral, so that both parties must fulfill obligations reciprocally towards each other (*e.g.*, a seller must deliver goods and the buyer must pay the price). Alternatively, it may be unilateral, so that one party is bound to fulfill obligations towards another without first receiving any return promise of performance (*e.g.*, a dog owner offers a reward for the return of her dog; someone may return the dog without promising to do so, thereby binding the owner to pay the reward).

2. **Implied-in-Fact Contracts.** An implied-in-fact contract is one arising as a matter of reason and justice from the acts, conduct, or circumstances surrounding a transaction, even though there are no formal or explicit writings. The obligation is still the manifested intent of the parties, but unlike an express contract, the terms of the implied-in-fact contract are inferred. For example, an implied-in-fact contract may arise when one person renders services to another at the other's request but without an express agreement as to the compensation to be paid. In such a case, a promise to pay the reasonable value of the services may be inferred. [*See* U.C.C. §1-201(3)]

3. **Implied-in-Law or Quasi Contracts.** An implied-in-law or quasi contract is not really a contract, but an obligation imposed upon a person out of fairness and equity regardless of her intent to be bound. This obligation even can be imposed in spite of an agreement between the parties. It is treated as if it were a contract.

D. ENFORCEMENT

Among the major functions of contract law are determining what promises should be enforced and to what extent they should be enforced. Once a contract exists, its breach may entitle the nonbreaching party to certain remedies, depending on the type of contract involved and the nature of the breach. The basic form of remedy is monetary compensation, although there are other remedies such as specific performance. These remedies are explored in detail later, but it is helpful to keep in mind the basic types of contract damages.

1. **Expectation.** A promisee may recover expectation damages if by reason of the breach he is worse off than he would have been if the promise had been performed. Such damages are intended to place the promisee in the position he would have been in had the promise been performed.

2. **Reliance.** A promisee may recover reliance damages if by reason of the breach he is worse off than he would have been if the promise had not been made; the damages are intended to put him back in the position he would have been in if the promise had not been made. The measure of such damages is typically out-of-pocket costs incurred in reliance on the promise and opportunity costs, such as the cost of substitute performance.

3. **Restitution.** When a promisee has conferred a benefit on the promisor, who then breaches, the promisee may recover the reasonable value of the benefit conferred.

II. THE BASIS OF CONTRACTUAL OBLIGATION: MUTUAL ASSENT AND CONSIDERATION

A. MUTUAL ASSENT

1. Intention to Be Bound: The Objective Theory of Contract.

a. Introduction. The intention to be bound by a contract is not a matter of subjective intent. The necessary intent is based on the party's objective manifestations. A party becomes bound by the reasonable interpretation of the party's words and actions.

1) Sufficient manifestation of assent. There is sufficient manifestation of assent whenever a party volitionally engages in conduct (words or acts) that he knows or should reasonably know the other party may interpret as an offer or acceptance. [Restatement (Second) of Contracts §21]

2) Written intention. Clearly expressed written intent cannot be contradicted by parol evidence, and a party cannot enforce its own interpretation on the plain meaning of the terms of the writing.

3) Rationale—protection of parties' reasonable expectations. Demands for security and certainty in business transactions, and the fundamental objective of protecting a party's reasonable expectations in relying on a promise, make it imperative that each contracting party be able to rely on the other party's apparent intentions without regard to his secret thoughts or mental reservations. [Restatement (Second) of Contracts §20]

b. Subjective intent contrary to writing--

Ray v. William G. Eurice & Bros., Inc., 93 A.2d 272 (Md. 1952).

Facts. The Rays (Ps) owned a lot and decided to build a house on it. Ps got an estimate from William G. Eurice & Bros., Inc. (D) for $16,000. During the course of negotiations, Ps provided seven pages of specifications prepared by Ps' architect. D suggested changes and eventually provided Ps an undated three-page proposal contract that contained specifications somewhat different from those Ps had provided. Ps' lawyer rewrote the contract and referenced five pages of specifications attached to the contract itself and dated February 14, 1951. Ps signed the contract at D's office at the same time D's president and secretary did. Ps got a loan and made other preparations. About a week before construction was supposed to start, D met with Ps and told them he would not build according to the specifications in the contract, which he claimed he had never seen. D refused to proceed and Ps sued. At trial, there was a dispute about whether the five pages of specifications were attached to the contract when it was signed. D claimed to believe the reference was to D's three-page specifications. The trial court concluded that there was a mistake because the parties had different sets of specifications in mind when they made the contract; hence, there was no real meeting of the minds. The court found for D. Ps appeal.

Issue. If one party to a contract is mistaken about the meaning of a contract term that is otherwise clear and unambiguous, can the mistaken party avoid enforcement of the contract?

Held. No. Judgment reversed.

♦ The evidence makes it difficult to believe that D would sign a contract to build a house without being sure what specifications applied to the project. The contract clearly references the five-page specifications, including the date. But even if D was mistaken, the mistake was unilateral. Ps intended that their specifications would be part of the contract and the contract so states.

♦ In the absence of fraud, duress, or mutual mistake, a party is bound by a contract if he has the capacity to read the written contract and actually does read and sign it. Unilateral mistake is not an exception to the rule.

♦ A party who manifests acceptance of the terms of a writing which he should reasonably understand to be a contract is bound by the contract. It does not matter that the party claims he actually intended to be bound by different terms.

♦ Because D wrongfully breached its contract, Ps are entitled to recover the difference in cost between the contract price and the actual cost to have someone else build the building. The evidence in this case supports an award to Ps of $5,993.40.

Comment. To some extent, the court held D to a high standard of self-protection because D had been in the construction business for a long time and should have known what specifications were involved before signing the contract.

---

2. **Offer and Aceptance in Bilateral Contracts.**

    a. **Offers compared with invitations to deal.** A statement is not an offer merely because it looks toward a bargain. Statements made in language or under circumstances indicating that the speaker only wants to begin negotiations are considered invitations to deal, or preliminary negotiations, rather than offers. For example, a price quotation is normally not an offer to sell but simply an invitation to the buyer to make an offer to purchase. When the circumstances indicate otherwise, however, a quotation may be elevated to the status of an offer.

1) Solicitation of offer is not an offer--

Lonergan v. Scolnick, 276 P.2d 8 (Cal. Dist. Ct. App. 1954).

Facts. Lonergan (P) inquired about land that Scolnick (D) had advertised in a newspaper. D sent P a form letter describing the property and stating the asking price of $2,500. P wrote back, asking for a legal description so he could make sure he had found the property and asking whether a certain bank would be acceptable to D as an escrow agent if P wanted to buy the land. On April 8, D wrote to P to verify that P had found the property, that the escrow agent was acceptable, and that P would have to act fast because D would sell to the first buyer and he expected one to make a deal in the next week. On April 12, D sold the property to a third party for $2,500. On April 14, P received D's letter. The next day, P sent a letter to D indicating that he would open escrow immediately and that D should send his deed to the escrow agent. On April 17, P gave $100 to the escrow agent and was ready and willing to deposit the balance at any time. Since D had sold the property, P sued for damages. The trial court found that the parties had not entered into a contract. P appeals.

Issue. May a person enter into a contract when the other party's communications were intended only as preliminary negotiations?

Held. No. Judgment affirmed.

♦   To have a contract, both parties must mutually agree to a specific thing. Normally, this is done by one party making an offer that the other party accepts. When the person to whom a communication is addressed knows or has reason to know that the person making it does not intend it as an expression of a fixed purpose until a further expression of assent is given, the person has not received an offer.

♦   In this case, D's letters were clearly intended to determine whether P was interested and to provide the requested information. At no time did D make a definite offer. On the contrary, D told P that D would take the first buyer that came along. D did not give P a right to act within a particular time, which is what an offer does.

2) Advertising--

Izadi v. Machado (Gus) Ford, Inc., 550 So. 2d 1135 (Fla. Dist. Ct. App. 1989).

Facts. Machado (Gus) Ford, Inc. (D) placed an ad in the newspaper. The top section of the ad stated, in large letters, BUY A NEW FORD & GET $3,000 MINIMUM TRADE-IN ALLOWANCE, followed by very small print stating that the offer applied only toward the purchase of two expensive models. The rest of the ad showed the list price of three less expensive cars with a deduction from each labeled "Any Trade Worth $3,000." Izadi (P), believing that the ad offered $3,000 as a minimum trade-in allowance for any car, regardless of its actual value, offered D the final price indicated in the ad for a new pickup truck. D declined to sell for that price, referring to the small print at the top of the ad. P sued for breach of contract, fraud, and violation of a misleading advertising statute. The trial court dismissed the complaint. P appeals.

Issue. May an advertiser be bound by the objective interpretation of its advertising, even where it did not intend that interpretation?

Held. Yes. Judgment reversed.

♦ P alleges that he accepted D's offer to allow $3,000 toward the purchase of the pickup for any vehicle P produced. His allegation is based on an objective reading of the entire advertisement, and is based on the theory that an enforceable contract arises from an offer contained in an advertisement. While this is a minority rule, it has been followed enough that it can apply in this case.

♦ D subjectively may not have intended for the ad to constitute a binding offer, but P is entitled to prove that an objective reading of the ad conveys an offer. P then accepted the offer when he offered the cash and the trade-in. This is all that is required to state a claim for breach of contract.

♦ P also has a breach of contract claim based on the "bait and switch" tactic. A binding offer may be implied from the very fact that deliberately misleading advertising intentionally leads the reader to the conclusion that one exists.

Comment. The court noted that P would have to show not only that an objective reading of the ad would constitute an offer, but also that he was in fact misled into a genuine belief that the offer had been made. P cannot simply take advantage of D's imprecise language. Note also that the traditional rule treats advertisements as invitations for offers, not offers. To be an offer, an advertisement must include language of commitment or an invitation to take action without further communication.

---

3) Real estate purchase offers and counteroffers--

Normile v. Miller, 326 S.E.2d 11 (N.C. 1985).

Facts. Miller (D) owned real estate that she listed for sale with Hawkins. Byer, another real estate agent, showed D's property to Normile and Kurniawan (Ps). Ps made an offer that specified it had to be accepted on or before 5:00 p.m. on August 5. Byer took the offer to Hawkins, who gave it to D. D made some changes in the earnest money deposit, the down payment, and other provisions. Hawkins then gave it to Byer, who presented it to Ps. Normile said he could not pay the earnest money deposit D wanted, and Byer thought P had rejected the counteroffer. Byer then helped Segal make an offer to purchase D's property that was similar to the terms of D's counteroffer to Ps. D accepted this offer during the day on August 5 and told P that she revoked her counteroffer. Before 5:00 p.m., Ps initialed D's counteroffer and delivered it along with the earnest money deposit. Ps then sought specific performance. The court awarded summary judgment to Segal, requiring D to sell the property to him. Ps appealed. The court of appeals affirmed. The North Carolina Supreme Court accepted discretionary review.

Issue. Does an acceptance period contained in an offer remain valid if the offeree makes a counteroffer that does not include an acceptance period?

Held. No. Judgment affirmed.

♦ Ps' initial offer controlled D's power of acceptance by limiting the duration of time for acceptance to 5:00 p.m. on August 5. When D made the counteroffer, she made a qualified or conditional acceptance, which could also be considered as a rejection of Ps' offer. Therefore, D did not accept Ps' original offer prior to the expiration of the time limit.

♦ Ps' time-for-acceptance provision did not become part of the terms of D's counteroffer. If Ps had accepted the counteroffer, there would have been a binding purchase contract. But D's counteroffer did not contain a promise or commitment to hold the counteroffer open for a specified period of time, and it did not reference Ps' original time limit. D's counteroffer was not irrevocable.

♦ A party cannot accept a counteroffer after it has been revoked. The evidence is clear that Ps did not accept D's counteroffer when Byer presented it to them. P claimed he had an option on the property until 5:00 p.m., but he was mistaken about this.

♦ When D accepted Segal's offer, D manifested her intention to revoke the previous counteroffer to Ps. An offer is freely revocable and can be countermanded by the offeror at any time before the offeree accepts it. D notified P that the property was sold before Ps attempted to accept the counteroffer. Ps' power to accept D's counteroffer was terminated by D's revocation of the counteroffer.

---

3. **Offer and Acceptance in Unilateral Contracts.**

    a. **Revocation of offers.** A revocation, which is a retraction of the offer by the offeror, normally terminates the offeree's power of acceptance—

provided that the offer has not already been accepted. Numerous problems can arise in determining when an offer can still be revoked.

b.   Revocability of offers for unilateral contracts. Since an offer for a unilateral contract may be accepted by performance, problems may arise when the offeror attempts to revoke the offer after performance has begun but before performance has been completed. A contract is formed by the offeree's full performance even though the offeror does not know at the time that performance has occurred. However, the offeror's contractual obligation is subject to the implied condition that he receive notice of the completed performance within a reasonable time. Thus, the basic problem is determining up to what time the offeror may revoke an offer for a unilateral contract.

c.   Traditional rule--

Petterson v. Pattberg, 161 N.E. 428 (N.Y. 1928).

Facts. Petterson, represented at trial by his executrix (P), had executed a promissory note to Pattberg (D), secured by a third mortgage on property owned by the deceased. D had offered in writing to discount the amount of the mortgage if it was paid on or before a specified date. The deceased went to D's home and told D that he was ready to pay, but D refused to accept the payment, indicating that he had already sold the note and mortgage to another party. The deceased needed to pay off the mortgage because he had sold the land to a third party free and clear of the mortgage. P sued D for damages. The trial court found for P. D appeals.

Issue. May an offer of a unilateral contract be revoked at any time prior to performance, even if the offeror knows that the offeree intends to perform?

Held. Yes. Judgment reversed.

♦   The offer of a unilateral contract may be revoked at any time prior to full performance of the act required as acceptance.

♦   D revoked the offer before P tendered payment.

♦   Even if P had tendered payment to D, only P's completed act of payment would constitute acceptance.

Dissent. If the completed act of payment were required, the only way P could have accepted D's offer would be if D further performed by accepting the money. Therefore, D's refusal to accept the money would prevent P from accepting D's offer. In light of the surrounding circumstances, D did not intend that the only method of acceptance was complete payment when he wrote the letter containing the offer. In this case, not only did P not complete payment before D's attempted revocation (*i.e.*, D's statement that he sold the mortgage to another), but P did not even tender payment. At that point, D only stated that he had "come to pay off the mortgage." However, if D was acting in good faith when he wrote the letter to P, he probably did not intend for P to make a tender without first stating that he had come to make the payment. Therefore, P formed a binding contract with D.

Comment. Modern rules do not permit revocation where there has been substantial part performance rendered by the offeree, but even under these rules the result in this case would be the same because the act required for acceptance was payment, and the revocation came before payment.

---

d. Part performance as acceptance of bonus offer--

Cook v. Coldwell Banker/Frank Laiben Realty Co., 967 S.W.2d 654 (Mo. Ct. App. 1998).

Facts. Cook (P) was a real estate agent who worked for Coldwell Banker/Frank Laiben Realty Co. (D) as an independent contractor. In March 1991, D held a sales meeting at which a bonus program was announced. All agents who earned $15,000 in commissions would receive an immediate $500 bonus, with higher bonuses paid on higher commissions. The higher bonuses would be earned over a year and would be paid at the end of the year. In April, P surpassed $15,000, and was paid her $500 bonus in September. By September, P had surpassed $32,400 in commissions. In September, however, D announced that the bonuses would be paid the following March instead of at the end of the year, which meant the agents would have to stay with D until March to get the bonus. P joined a different company in January, and D told her she would not get her bonus, which by then was over $17,000. P demanded payment, but D refused. P sued for breach of contract. At trial, the court denied D's motion for a directed verdict, and the jury found for P. D appeals.

Issue. May an offeror revoke an offer for a unilateral contract if the offeree has already given part of the requested performance?

Held. No. Judgment affirmed.

♦   D claims that P failed to establish a reasonable inference that P tendered consideration to support D's offer of a bonus, or that P accepted D's offer of a bonus. P did provide evidence of a unilateral contract offered by D to pay a bonus. P also provided evidence of D's attempt to revoke the original offer and require instead that agents remain with D until March of the following year.

♦   A unilateral contract arises when performance is based on the will or pleasure of one of the parties. The promisor does not receive a promise as consideration, but receives a performance from the promisee as consideration. Thus, an offer to make a unilateral contract is accepted when the requested performance is rendered.

♦   A promise to pay a bonus in return for continued employment is an offer for a unilateral contract. When the employee performs by continuing to work, the offer is accepted. P could have terminated her relationship with D at any time and did not have to earn the specified level of commissions. D's bonus offer induced P to stay with D through the year and earn the high level of commissions. P thereby accepted D's offer.

♦   D claims P had not yet accepted D's first offer when the second offer was made, and when she left before March, P failed to accept the second offer. An offeror is entitled to withdraw an offer at any time prior to performance, but not when the offeree has made substantial performance. An offer for a unilateral contract necessarily includes a subsidiary promise that if part of the requested performance is given, the offeror will not revoke the offer. Besides, by September, P had earned enough commissions to make her eligible for the offered bonus.

---

e.   **Parties' conduct creating a contract--**

Harlow & Jones, Inc. v. Advance Steel Co., 424 F. Supp. 770 (E.D. Mich. 1976).

Facts. On July 2, Advance Steel Co.'s (D's) president told VanAs, an independent steel broker for Harlow & Jones, Inc. (P), that D was interested in purchasing 1,000 tons of steel from a shipment to be made during September-October. VanAs relayed the terms to P that same day. On July 9, P mailed D a sales form confirming the sale with shipment from Europe during September-October. P ordered the steel to cover the sale to D. D never signed or returned the sales order; instead, D sent P a purchase order, which P never signed or returned. The steel was sent in three shipments, the last of which left on November 14 and arrived in Detroit on November 27. D rejected the last shipment, claiming that it was a late delivery. P rejected D's cancellation. P eventually sold the steel at a loss. P sues, claiming that D breached the contract.

Issue. In a contract for the sale and purchase of steel, may an oral contract arise from the parties' discussions even when neither party exchanges written documents provided by the other?

Held. Yes. Judgment for P.

♦   The parties argue over the impact of their respective forms, neither of which specified a delivery date, but both of which specified a shipment date of "September-October." The evidence indicates that the parties formed an oral contract through telephone conversations between D's president and VanAs during the week of July 2, before either P or D sent written forms. The parties' conduct reflects the common understanding that the sale was agreed upon.

♦ It is not clear exactly when the binding contract was formed, but the oral negotiations left both parties believing and acting as though there was a contract. The written forms each party sent were therefore merely confirmatory memoranda that substantially agreed. The written forms contained the same price terms, weight and grade specifications, and shipment date.

♦ The evidence shows that in steel importing trade usage, steel shipped in September or October would arrive by October or November. Due to contingencies that P claims were unanticipated and out of P's control, P's final shipment left Europe in November, which was later than agreed upon. However, it arrived before the end of November, which was within the parties' agreement, according to trade usage. Therefore, P's breach did not result in a material delay.

B. CONSIDERATION

1. **Defining Consideration.** "Consideration" is the inducement to a contract. It is a benefit received by the promisor or a detriment incurred by the promisee. It arises in an agreed-to exchange and may consist of an act, a forbearance to act, or a mere promise to act. Analysis of consideration problems reveals that in every case, the parties must have *bargained* for something of *legal value* for there to be a legally sufficient consideration and thus a binding contract.

2. **Rationale for Enforcing Promises.** Private parties organize and pursue their private ventures through arrangements with one another. Frequently, these arrangements require one party to perform before the other; the former would have confidence in performing only with some assurance that the other party will likewise perform. This assurance is given through a promise, and because society has an interest in seeing that such private arrangements are made, society enforces private promises that meet established criteria. One of the most critical of these criteria is the bargain element.

3. **Sufficiency and Nature of Consideration.** Sufficient consideration is present only when each party to the contract has intended to secure something from the other party that he was otherwise not legally entitled to; *i.e.*, each must be bargaining for something from the other party, no matter how nominal this may seem to other, outside parties. The element of bar-

gain assures that, at least when the contract is formed, both parties see an advantage in contracting for the anticipated performance.

    a.   **Examples of benefit or detriment.** Legal consideration may be either: (i) a right, interest, profit, or benefit accruing to the promisor; or (ii) a forbearance, detriment, loss, or responsibility given, suffered, or undertaken by the promisee. The courts infer a legal detriment whenever a party obliges himself through a bargain to perform in a certain manner, even if the performance is not detrimental in the ordinary sense of the term.

    1)   **Abstention from legal conduct--**

Hamer v. Sidway, 27 N.E. 256 (N.Y. 1891).

Facts. Decedent promised his nephew that if he, the nephew, would refrain from drinking, using tobacco, swearing, and playing cards or billiards for money until the age of 21, decedent would pay him $5,000. Upon reaching 21, the nephew informed decedent that he had kept the bargain. Decedent reaffirmed his obligation but retained the funds until the nephew would be capable of taking care of them. Decedent then died without paying. The nephew assigned his claim to Hamer (P), who sued Sidway (D), the executor. The trial court held for P, but was reversed on appeal. P appeals.

Issue. Does a promisee's abstention from legal but harmful conduct constitute legal and sufficient consideration for a promise by the promisor to pay money?

Held. Yes. Judgment reversed.

♦   D claims the nephew suffered no detriment or loss, but a real benefit in abstaining from these vices; enforcing the contract would confer a double benefit on one party. However, a waiver of any legal rights at the request of another party (the promisor) is sufficient consideration for a promise.

♦   The nephew clearly had a legal right to engage in these vices, and his waiver of that right, his voluntary restriction of his lawful freedom, is legal and sufficient consideration for the promise. In addition, we cannot say that decedent (the promisor) was not benefited in any legal sense by his nephew's abstention from these vices.

Comments.

♦   A bargain promise is not always easily distinguished from a conditional donative promise. For example, A promises to provide B a hotel room if B comes to Los Angeles. There is no bargain; B's coming to Los Angeles was merely a condition to fulfillment of the gift. It was not the bargained-for price of A's making the promise. The distinguishing test is how the parties view the condition. In *Hamer*, abstention was the price of the promise, so there was a bargain.

- Certain promises must be in writing to be enforceable. This principle is governed by the Statute of Frauds.

---

2) Benefit conferred as consideration--

Pennsy Supply, Inc. v. American Ash Recycling Corp., 895 A.2d 595 (Pa. Super. Ct. 2006).

Facts. As a subcontractor, Pennsy Supply, Inc. (P) contracted to pave driveways and a parking lot. The Project Specifications permitted the use of AggRite as a base aggregate and noted that American Ash Recycling Corp. (D) had AggRite available for free on a first come, first served basis. P obtained 11,000 tons of AggRite from D and used it in the paving work. Later, the pavement developed cracking, and P was required to remedy the defective work. D refused P's request to remove and dispose of the AggRite. P spent over $250,000 in remedial work, plus over $130,000 to dispose of the AggRite, which was a hazardous waste material. P sued D for breach of contract (as well as for breach of warranty and promissory estoppel). The trial court granted D's motion to dismiss the complaint. P appeals.

Issue. If a party obtains construction material for free from another party, and the second party incurs a benefit from avoiding disposal costs of the construction material, may the second party be held liable for breach of contract?

Held. Yes. Judgment reversed and case remanded.

- The trial court held that there was no agreement between P and D because of lack of consideration, that P merely received a conditional gift from D, and that the parties never bargained about disposal costs.

- Consideration is required to have an enforceable contract; it consists of a benefit to the promisor or a detriment to the promisee. In distinguishing between consideration and a condition, an important factor is whether the occurrence of the condition would benefit the promisor, because this would support an inference that the occurrence was requested as consideration.

- In this case, P alleges that D actively promoted the use of AggRite as material to be used in paving projects and provided the material free of charge because it wanted to avoid incurring the disposal costs it would otherwise have to pay. P further claims that by using D's AggRite, P saved D thousands of dollars in disposal costs.

- These allegations must be deemed true in deciding to grant a motion to dismiss. They could fairly be interpreted to show that D's promise to supply AggRite for free induced P to assume the detriment of taking the material, and it was precisely this detriment that induced D to make the promise to provide the free AggRite for the project.

♦ P did not specifically allege that the parties bargained about D's avoidance of disposal costs, but such an actual negotiation is not required to have consideration. All that is required is that the promise and the consideration be reciprocal.

---

b. **Donative promises.** A donative promise is a promise to make a gift. There is no bargain involved; the person making the promise acts out of affection, charity, or some other personal motivation, without requiring a promise or performance in return.

   1) **General rule.** Such promises are generally not enforceable; because there is no bargain element, the likely injury that would result from the breach of a donative promise is relatively slight. The law does not provide a remedy for a lost hope, and the promisor is unlikely to have been enriched at the promisee's expense. There are exceptions to the rule, such as when the promisee has detrimentally relied on the promise. From a practical standpoint, the lack of bargain and consideration make proof of simple donative promises difficult; *i.e.*, a claimant could easily make up a promise by another to make a gift.

   2) **Promissory note evidencing future gift--**

Dougherty v. Salt, 125 N.E. 94 (N.Y. 1919).

Facts. Dougherty (P), an eight-year-old boy, received a promissory note from his aunt, payable at or before her death. The aunt gave P the note because she loved him and wanted to take care of him. The form on which the note was written contained the words "value received." Upon the aunt's death, P brought suit on the note. A verdict for P was set aside and his complaint dismissed. The appellate division reversed. Salt (D), the executor, appeals.

Issue. May a voluntary promise of a gift to be made in the future, given without consideration to the promisor, be enforced by the promisee?

Held. No. Judgment reversed.

♦ The evidence permits only one interpretation; the promise is unenforceable because it was intended only as a gift. The aunt received nothing from P that could be characterized as "consideration."

♦ It is clear that P was not a creditor, nor was he dealt with as one. The words on the form are meaningless when no value was actually received by the aunt.

Comments.

♦ The basis for the rule denying enforcement of simple donative promises is that the courts do not feel bound to help a person who attempts to get something for nothing. Another rationale is that a promisee who gives nothing for a promise is no worse off when the promise is broken than he was before it was given.

♦ Although donative promises are not enforceable, the gift, once made, is; *i.e.*, a person who makes the gift by delivering possession cannot later recover possession.

---

c. **Adequacy of consideration.** Any performance that is bargained for is consideration, regardless of whether the values exchanged are equivalent. [*See* Restatement (Second) §§71, 72, 79] However, a gross inadequacy of consideration may be evidence of fraud, mistake, duress, or undue influence.

  1) **Judicial review of consideration.** In most cases, the courts do not examine whether a bargained-for price is commensurate in value with the performance promised. Courts do not like to value acts, and hence, even if minimal, acts are usually sufficient consideration. So long as there is no fraud or deception, "the slightest consideration is sufficient to support the most onerous obligation." [Mandel v. Liebman, 100 N.E.2d 149 (N.Y. 1951)] However, if the contract involves an exchange of assets whose monetary value is easily determined, the courts may consider the adequacy of the consideration.

  2) **Exceptions.** Despite the general rule, in certain types of cases the courts have held that no consideration is present even though a bargain had apparently been reached. These include:

    a) Bargains between members of a *family* relating to their ongoing relationship;

    b) Transactions that are *bargains in form but not in substance*, where neither party really views each promised performance as the price of the other;

    c) Bargains involving the *surrender of a legal claim*, if the claim is unreasonable or dishonestly asserted;

d)   Apparent bargains involving an *illusory promise*; and

e)   Bargains involving a *preexisting legal obligation*.

3)   Exchange of different currencies--

Batsakis v. Demotsis, 226 S.W.2d 673 (Tex. Ct. App. 1949).

Facts. During World War II, Batsakis (P), a Greek resident, loaned Demotsis (D), another Greek resident, 500,000 drachmae, which at the time was worth $25. D gave P a written note to repay $2,000 in United States currency. P sued on the note and the court gave a judgment to P of $750, the value of 500,000 drachmae at the time of trial. P appeals.

Issue. May a court inquire into the sufficiency of consideration to determine whether the parties received equal value?

Held. No. Judgment reversed.

◆   The parties had a valid contract at the time of the agreement. D accepted 500,000 drachmae for a promise to later repay $2,000 in United States dollars.

◆   The courts do not examine the contract between the parties to determine whether the consideration received by each side was equivalent. Nor was there a failure of consideration, because D got exactly what she contracted for.

◆   The trial court should have given judgment to P for the full amount of the note.

Comment. Normally, a court does not inquire into the adequacy of consideration because public policy allows the parties to make their own contract, each party determining what is valuable to him. However, even though the adequacy of consideration is immaterial as to formation of a contract, it may be relevant to issues of capacity, fraud, duress, etc.

---

d.   **Past action and moral obligations.**

1)   **Introduction.** The cases are split as to whether a promise to pay a moral obligation is enforceable when it arises out of a benefit previously conferred upon the promisor. However, the modern tendency is to hold that such a promise is enforceable, at least up to the value of the benefit conferred.

2)   **Moral obligations.** A promise is said to be given for moral or past consideration when the promisor is motivated by some past event

which inspires the promisor to make his promise. Usually (but not invariably), the past event is a transaction of some sort between the promisor and the promisee which benefited the promisor and placed him under a moral obligation to the promisee. Such promise is similar to a simple donative promise, differing principally with regard to the promisor's motive; *i.e.*, in the case of moral or past consideration, the promisor's motive is to discharge a preexisting moral obligation, while in the case of a simple donative promise (*e.g.*, I will give you $100 on your next birthday), such motive need not be present.

3) **Past consideration--**

Plowman v. Indian Refining Co., 20 F. Supp. 1 (E.D. Ill. 1937).

Facts. Plowman and other employees (Ps) had worked for many years for Indian Refining Co. (D). D's general manager told Ps that D would pay them one-half of their then-current wages for the rest of their lives. The consideration was the existing employment relationship plus D's desire to provide for the future welfare of Ps, as well as the requirement that Ps come to D's office to get their checks each payday. Ps were retained on the payroll but were not required to render further services. D sent Ps a letter describing the arrangement, although the letter said nothing about how long the payments would continue. About a year later, D notified Ps that the payments were being terminated. Ps sued. D claims the payments were gratuitous and without consideration, and besides, were not properly authorized by D. Ps claim that D ratified the original agreement and should be estopped from denying its validity.

Issue. Is a company's promise to pay employees a retirement salary enforceable where the only consideration cited was the long and faithful service of the employees?

Held. No. Judgment for D.

♦   Assuming D's general manager did make the alleged promise to Ps, the disposition of the case is a matter for legal analysis only. There was no evidence that D's general manager was authorized to make the promise to Ps. The fact that D made the payments to Ps for about a year cannot be considered ratification of the retirement agreement because D's duly authorized officers only knew that Ps were on the payroll, not that they had stopped working.

♦   Ps provided no consideration for the promise. Past consideration in the form of Ps' long and faithful service is not effective as consideration; it was given before the promise was made, so the promise was not bargained for.

♦   Some courts have recognized the validity of moral consideration, but the majority approach rejects this view on the ground that moral consideration is contrary in character to actual consideration. If the moral duty is not also a legal duty, it cannot constitute legal consideration.

♦ The fact that Ps visited D's office to get their checks cannot constitute consideration because this visit was a benefit to Ps, not a detriment.

♦ The promise to pay Ps for the rest of their lives was a gratuitous arrangement without consideration, and is void as a contract.

Comment. The court noted the public policy considerations in favor of retirement payments, but concluded that it could not enforce public policy where there was no valid contract.

C. ISSUES IN APPLYING THE CONCEPT OF MUTUAL ASSENT

1. Limits on Offeror's Power to Revoke.

a. **Promissory estoppel—detrimental reliance on a promise.** Within limits, detrimental action or forbearance by the promisee, in reliance on a promise, constitutes a *substitute* for consideration and renders the promise enforceable to the extent explained below. The promisee's detrimental reliance is deemed sufficient reason to *estop* the promisor from asserting the lack of consideration.

b. **Making offers irrevocable.** For similar reasons, a growing number of courts hold that an offeree's foreseeable, detrimental reliance on an offer will serve as a substitute for consideration, so as to create an option and prevent the offeror from thereafter revoking the offer for at least a reasonable time.

c. **Traditional view not recognizing reliance--**

James Baird Co. v. Gimbel Bros., Inc., 64 F.2d 344 (2d Cir. 1933).

Facts. Gimbel Bros. (D) estimated the cost to do a linoleum job on a large project and sent a letter to 30 contractors indicating that it was offering to supply enough linoleum to do the job at a certain price for "prompt acceptance after the general contract has been awarded." James Baird Co. (P) used D's price in making its bid. The same day, D learned of a substantial mistake in its calculation and sent P a withdrawal notice by telegraph, which P did not receive until after making its bid. Two days later, P's bid was accepted, and several days after that, P accepted D's original bid. D refused to perform and P sued for breach. The trial court found for D. P appeals.

Issue. May an offeree's reliance on an offer act as a substitute for consideration, thereby making the offer irrevocable?

Held. No. Judgment affirmed.

♦ P did not accept D's offer before D revoked it. Promissory estoppel is available where a promise is made without anticipation of a return promise or performance but where the promisee has acted in reliance on the promise nonetheless.

♦ In the case at bar, D's offer anticipated P's acceptance (not P's bid) and could not become a promise until accepted by P.

Comment. This case represents the old rule in contractor-subcontractor bid cases, where reliance did not serve as a substitute for consideration. The following case illustrates the modern rule.

---

d. Modern view recognizing reliance--

Drennan v. Star Paving Co., 333 P.2d 757 (Cal. 1958).

Facts. Star Paving Co. (D), a subcontractor, submitted a bid on a public school building to Drennan (P), the general contractor. In his bid, P had to give all subcontractors' names and their prices. P's bid was accepted. Shortly thereafter, D told P that its bid was underestimated, and it refused to perform. P then contracted with another paving company at a higher price and sued D for the difference. The trial court found for P. D appeals.

Issue. Where the general contractor relied on the subcontractor's bid and is unable to find another subcontractor for the same amount of money, does this reliance act as a substitute for consideration?

Held. Yes. Judgment affirmed.

♦ P received a clear and definite offer. P's reliance was reasonable and foreseeable by D, and P relied to its detriment.

♦ P's reliance is sufficient to imply a subsidiary promise by D not to revoke D's offer.

Comment. Modern cases hold that if reliance was "reasonable and foreseeable" and if the reliance produced detriment, then the subcontractor will be bound to his bid. This court implied a promise not to revoke an offer.

---

e.   Motive separate from consideration--

Berryman v. Kmoch, 559 P.2d 790 (Kan. 1977).

Facts. Berryman (P) owned real estate. Kmoch (D) was a real estate broker. D met P and obtained a 120-day option agreement from P that allowed D to purchase P's property for a specified price. The agreement recited that the option was granted "for $10 and other valuable consideration," but the $10 was never paid. About a month later, P called D and asked to be released from the option agreement, but they never settled on anything specific. A month after that, D decided to purchase the land. D's banker told him that P had already sold the property. D then recorded the option agreement and told P he was exercising the option. P filed a declaratory judgment action to have the option contract declared null and void. The trial court entered summary judgment for P. D appeals.

Issue. Do the efforts of an option holder to try to sell the optioned property constitute consideration for the option?

Held. No. Judgment affirmed.

- ◆   An option to purchase land is binding only if there is consideration, just like any other contract. In the absence of consideration, the option is no more than a continuing offer to sell that may be withdrawn at any time prior to acceptance.

- ◆   D claims that promissory estoppel should make the option enforceable, but there was no conduct in this case that could reasonably be expected as a result of extending the option promise. D merely claims he spent time, effort, and expense in trying to get other investors to purchase the property. The option did not obligate D to do anything and there was no basis for promissory estoppel.

- ◆   D claims that P must have given the option expecting something in return from D. However, D did not promise to do anything, and he was not required to do anything. If P expected D to raise the money to pay for the land, this would merely be P's motive for signing the option agreement. Motives or inducements to enter an agreement are not consideration for the contract. Desire to obtain consideration is not consideration. D's time and money spent trying to sell the property is not consideration to P.

- ◆   Revocation of an option can take place when (i) the offeror takes definite action inconsistent with an intention to enter into the proposed contract, and (ii) the offeree acquires reliable information to that effect. In this case, P told D directly that he wanted to be released from the option, which could have been a revocation. It is clear that once D's banker told him about P's sale of the property to a third party, D's power of acceptance was immediately terminated.

Comments.

- ◆ Some courts have held that a purchaser's efforts to obtain a loan to buy the property may constitute consideration, at least where the option contains language to that effect.

- ◆ There is a split on the application of the "mailbox rule" to options, with some courts requiring an acceptance to be actually received to be effective, while others require merely a deposit in the mail.

---

f.   Extent of promise required--

Pop's Cones, Inc. v. Resorts International Hotel, Inc., 704 A.2d 1321 (N.J. Super. Ct. 1998).

Facts. Pop's Cones, Inc. (P) was a franchisee of TCBY Systems, Inc., a national frozen yogurt franchisor. Resorts International Hotel, Inc. (D) operated a casino hotel that leased retail space in prime areas. P and D discussed having P move its store from its existing location to one of D's locations. P conducted a market test and the parties discussed formalizing a lease. In August, P gave D a written proposal for payment of seven percent of P's net monthly sales, with a six-year renewable term. In mid-September, P asked about the status of the proposal. P also told D that it had to give notice to its landlord by October 1. D told P that they were 95% there and told P to give notice to the landlord and plan on moving. P notified its landlord and packed up its store. Negotiations dragged on until December, when D made a counteroffer for a three-year renewable term. D continued delaying until January 30, when P's lawyer received a letter from D saying that D was withdrawing its offer. P sued for damages, claiming promissory estoppel. The trial court granted summary judgment for D. P appeals.

Issue. Is a simple promise to do something, combined with encouragement that the promisee take detrimental action in reliance on the promise, sufficient to support a claim based on promissory estoppel?

Held. Yes. Judgment reversed.

- ◆ The first element of promissory estoppel, as established in prior cases, is a clear and definite promise by the promisor. The trial court relied on *Malaker Corp. Stockholders Protective Commission v. First Jersey National Bank*, 395 A.2d 222 (N.J. App. Div. 1978), which required an express promise of a clear and definite nature. In the absence of such a promise, the court held that it was unnecessary to consider the remaining elements of promissory estoppel.

- ◆ The *Malaker* formula has been relaxed in more recent cases. It is no longer necessary to provide evidence of such a definite promise to establish a prima facie case of promissory estoppel.

- The better approach is to focus on the need to avoid injustice. In this case, for example, D knew that P had to renew its existing lease by October 1. D told P that they were close to finalizing the lease, and that P should not renew its old lease but plan on moving. P relied on these representations to its detriment.

- A jury could conclude from this evidence that D, as promisor, should reasonably have expected to induce P's action or forbearance. A jury would have to determine whether P's reliance was reasonable.

---

2. **The U.C.C. Firm Offer.**

   a. **Introduction.** Case law generally provides that a firm offer, meaning an offer that by its terms is to remain open for a specified period, can be revoked before its expiration, just as an ordinary offer. The rationale is that no consideration was given for the promise, so the promise to hold the offer open is not binding.

      1) **Options.** One exception to the general rule is where consideration is given for the promise to hold the offer open. This is an option agreement.

      2) **Nominal consideration.** Most courts, and the Restatement, make a firm offer irrevocable if it recites a nominal consideration, if the offer is in writing and proposes a fair exchange within a reasonable time.

      3) **Reliance.** If the offeror should have foreseen that the offer would induce reliance, the offer is irrevocable.

   b. **Statutory firm offers.** The U.C.C. adds a new type of firm offer. Section 2-205 of the U.C.C. provides that a signed, written offer by a merchant to buy or sell goods is not revocable for lack of consideration if it gives assurance that it will be held open. The irrevocability period cannot exceed three months. This rule applies to offers by buyers and sellers equally. Note that U.C.C. section 2-205 does not require reliance.

3. **Qualified Acceptance and the Battle of Forms.**

   a. **Introduction.** The ideal negotiation process involves a give and take that ultimately leads to a meeting of the minds. Frequently, however, the parties struggle to get to that point. It is common for an offeror to propose terms that are close to what the offeree can accept, but not quite. In this situation, the offeree may give a qualified or conditional acceptance.

1) **General rule.** The general rule is that a purported acceptance that adds to or changes the terms of the offer (a qualified or conditional acceptance) terminates the offeree's power of acceptance. It is deemed a counteroffer, which is an offer that the original offeror can accept or reject. This has been called the "mirror image" rule.

2) **Battle of forms.** Modern business transactions are commonly documented with preprinted forms exchanged by the parties, such as a buyer's Purchase Order or a seller's Sales Order. Typically, each party's forms contain different terms; each wants terms most favorable to itself. An exchange of such forms would not result in a contract, so a seller would have no duty to ship goods. If the seller does elect to ship goods, the law would imply acceptance by the seller of the last form sent; *i.e.*, the last form was a counteroffer, and shipment and acceptance of goods was considered acceptance of the counteroffer. This was called the "last shot" rule because the last form sent by either party controlled the terms of the transaction.

3) **U.C.C. rule.** U.C.C. section 2-207(1) changes the common law mirror image rule so that a definite and seasonable expression of acceptance functions as an acceptance even though it states terms additional to or different from those offered or agreed upon, unless acceptance is expressly made conditional on assent to the additional or different terms. The effect of U.C.C. section 2-207 depends on whether the parties are merchants.

   a) **Nonmerchants.** If the parties are not merchants, the contract terms are those in the offer, and any additional or different terms are not part of the contract.

   b) **Merchants.** The rules are more complex for merchants, depending on whether the terms are different or additional.

      (1) **Different terms.** Most courts have held that different terms are not part of the agreement and they cancel each other out, so that the contract terms are only those to which both parties agreed, supplemented by terms implied by the U.C.C.. Some courts treat different terms the same as additional terms.

      (2) **Additional terms.** Additional terms are part of the contract unless: (i) the offer expressly limits acceptance to the terms of the offer, (ii) the additional terms materially alter the terms of the contract, or (iii) the offeror objects to the additional terms by reasonable notification to the offeree.

b.   U.C.C. inapplicable to contract for services--

Princess Cruises, Inc. v. General Electric Co., 143 F.3d 828 (4th Cir. 1998).

Facts. Princess Cruises, Inc. (P) scheduled one of its ships for routine inspection and repairs. P gave General Electric Co. (D) a purchase order ("PO") for services and parts totaling $260,000. The terms and conditions provided that D could accept the PO through acknowledgment or performance. Some time after D received the PO, D faxed P a final price quotation ("FPQ") for $231,925. This one rejected the terms of P's PO, rejected liquidated damages, limited D's liability to repair or replace defective goods, and disclaimed any liability for consequential damages, lost profits, or lost revenue. P accepted D's FPQ. When P's ship arrived for inspection, D noticed rust on the rotor. While D serviced the rotor, it became unbalanced and D was unable to correct the problem in time for P to use the ship on a 10-day cruise. P paid D the full contract price for the work, but claimed the continued vibration damaged the ship, forcing additional repairs and another cancellation. P sued for breach of contract, breach of express warranty, breach of implied maritime warranty, and negligence. The trial court granted D's motion for summary judgment as to negligence. At the end of P's case, the court denied D's motion for judgment as a matter of law. The judge instructed the jury on U.C.C. section 2-207, allowing the jury to imply various warranties and rights to recover consequential damages. The jury awarded P $4,577,743. D appeals.

Issue. Do the concepts behind the U.C.C. with respect to contract interpretation apply to a contract for services?

Held. No. Judgment reversed and case remanded.

- ◆   Because the case involves work on a ship, the applicable law is admiralty law, not the U.C.C. In admiralty, a maritime contract for goods and services is subject to the same inquiry as a land-based mixed contract. The first step is determining whether the predominant purpose of the transaction is the sale of goods.

- ◆   The U.C.C. applies to cases in which the predominant purpose of the transaction is the furnishing of goods. This can be determined from: (i) the language of the contract; (ii) the nature of the business of the supplier; and (iii) the intrinsic worth of the materials. In this case, the contract clearly was principally concerned with the rendering of services. Parts were incidental to the services. The contract came from D's service engineering department. Finally, although the cost of materials was not specified in the contract, P's claim is based on D's deficient services.

- ◆   In admiralty, when no federal statute or well-established rule of admiralty exists, admiralty law may look to the common law or to state law. Most states refer to common-law principles to interpret contracts for services, so the common law should apply to this case.

♦   At common law, an acceptance that varies the terms of an offer is a counteroffer that rejects the original offer. D's FPQ altered P's PO, so D's FPQ became a counteroffer rejecting P's PO. P accepted D's FPQ. Therefore, the contract consists of what was in D's FPQ. Under the terms of D's FPQ only, P's recovery was limited to the contract price and D could not be held liable for consequential damages. Since the jury award far exceeded these limits, they must have improperly considered some other contract. On remand, the court shall enter judgment for P for the $231,925 amount of the contract.

Comment. Note that under common law, a varying acceptance is only a counteroffer. The terms of the original offer are not part of the parties' contract. This is the "mirror image" rule. The other rule, called the "last shot" rule, provides that the last form sent is the one that applies.

---

c.   Failure to make conditional acceptance clear--

Brown Machine, Inc. v. Hercules, Inc., 770 S.W.2d 416 (Mo. Ct. App. 1989).

Facts. Brown Machine, Inc. (P) sold a T-100 trim press to Hercules, Inc. (D) that was used to make Cool Whip bowls. During sales negotiations, D's engineer asked P's sales manager to send D a quote for a trim press. P submitted a proposal that included a term on liability that required D to indemnify P from all claims arising out of the use of the press. D's purchasing agent gave P a verbal purchase order ("PO"). D subsequently sent a written PO that contained no indemnity provision but provided that it limited acceptance to the terms stated in the PO and rejected any additional or different terms proposed by P. P then sent D an "Order Acknowledgement" ("OA") that required D to notify P if the conditions it contained were not in accordance with D's understanding. The OA included the indemnity clause. Later, one of D's employees was injured while operating the trim press. He sued P. P demanded that D defend the lawsuit based on the indemnity clause. D refused. P eventually settled the employee's lawsuit, but sued D for indemnification. The jury found for P and awarded P nearly $160,000 in damages. D appeals.

Issue. If a response to an offer contains additional or different terms but does not expressly make acceptance conditional on agreement with those terms, does it act as a counteroffer?

Held. No. Judgment reversed.

♦   The general rule recognizes that a price quotation is not an offer, but merely an invitation to enter negotiations. However, if the price quote is detailed enough, it can create a power of acceptance such that mere assent to the quotation may make a contract.

♦ In this case, P's quotation was not a firm offer to contract, but merely an offer to enter into negotiations, because it provided that D's acceptance was not binding upon P until P acknowledged the acceptance. Even if P's proposal had been an offer, it was only effective for 30 days, and D's PO was dated after the expiration of the quotation.

♦ D's PO is the actual offer, since orders are normally considered as offers to purchase and P's previous document, the quotation, had expired by the time D issued the PO. D would only be liable if P's OA containing the indemnity provision constitutes a counteroffer.

♦ Under U.C.C. section 2-207(1), an offeree's response to an offer is a valid acceptance of the offer even if it contains terms additional to, or different from, the terms of the offer unless acceptance is expressly made conditional on the offeror's agreement with the additional or different terms. In such a case, the response operates as a counteroffer, not an acceptance.

♦ Nothing in P's OA reflects P's unwillingness to proceed unless it obtained D's assent to the additional and different terms the OA contained, including the indemnity provision. P's OA was not "expressly made conditional" upon D's acceptance of those terms.

♦ Because P's OA was not a counteroffer, it operated as an acceptance with additional or different terms. Under U.C.C. section 2-207(2), additional terms become part of the contract unless the offer expressly limits acceptance to the terms of the offer. D's PO did expressly limit acceptance to the terms of D's offer, so P's additional terms, including the indemnity clause, did not become part of the contract.

♦ There is no evidence that D expressly assented to the indemnity clause. Although P's OA required D to advise P about any specifications and terms and conditions that were not in accordance with D's understanding, D merely objected to one and said all other specifications were correct. D never said anything about the terms and conditions, and express assent cannot be presumed by silence or mere failure to object.

---

4. **The "Agreements to Agree."**

   a. **Introduction.** A basic rule of contract law is that an agreement is binding only if it is sufficiently definite to allow a court to give it a certain meaning. If the contract is uncertain, it cannot be enforced. The negotiation process is a continuum, and if the parties stop negotiation short of a definitive contract, but they begin performance anyway, the courts need to determine whether there is a binding contract or merely an agreement to agree. Some terms are essential to a contract, so that, in their absence, there can be no contract. In other cases, the question may be whether one of the parties intended to be bound by the negotiations.

b.   Uncertain material term--

Walker v. Keith, 382 S.W.2d 198 (Ky. Ct. App. 1964).

Facts. Walker (P) leased a small lot from Keith (D) for 10 years at $100 per month. The lease gave P the option of renewing the lease for an additional 10-year period, with rent to be agreed upon according to "the comparative basis of rental values as of the date of the renewal with rental values at this time reflected by the comparative business conditions of the two periods." At the end of the 10-year lease, P wished to renew but the parties were unable to agree on the rent. P sued D to specifically enforce the option to extend the lease and to have the court establish the rent. The trial court granted P specific performance and set rent at $125. D appeals.

Issue. Is an option enforceable if the provision for determining rent is so indefinite that the parties cannot be held to have agreed to the essential terms of the renewal?

Held. No. Judgment reversed.

♦   The renewal provision neither fixes rent nor establishes any specific method of determining it. Although the contract sets a standard of "comparative business conditions," it is not sufficiently certain since the court does not know if the parties meant local conditions, national conditions, or conditions affecting P's particular business.

♦   The fact that the parties themselves never were able to agree on rent evidences that only an agreement to agree existed. In order for a contract to be formed, the law requires substantial certainty as to material terms upon which the parties have agreed. Because rent is a material term of a lease and the parties did not agree to a substantially certain rent or method of determining rent, no enforceable contract was made.

c.   Letter of intent--

Quake Construction, Inc. v. American Airlines, Inc., 565 N.E.2d 990 (Ill. 1990).

Facts. American Airlines, Inc. (D) hired Jones to expand D's facilities at O'Hare Airport. Jones invited Quake Construction, Inc. (P) to bid on the project. Jones orally told P that P had been awarded the contract. P required a written contract before getting information from P's subcontractors, so Jones sent P a letter of intent ("LOI") confirming that P had been selected and outlining the terms of the project. The LOI reserved to Jones the right to cancel the LOI if the parties could not agree on a fully executed contract. The parties never signed a written contract. At a subsequent meeting, Jones told P that P was the contractor for the project, but right after the meeting, D told P that P's involvement was terminated. P sued to recover its preparation costs and loss of anticipated profits. The trial court dismissed the complaint. The appellate court reversed, finding the cancellation clause in the LOI to be ambiguous. D appeals.

Issue. May a letter of intent be an enforceable contract even if it contains a clause allowing one party to cancel it if the parties do not reach a written agreement?

Held. Yes. Judgment affirmed and case remanded.

♦ Even where the parties intend to execute a formal agreement in the future, prior agreements are not necessarily mere negotiations. If the parties intend that a letter of intent be contractually binding, it may be enforced as a contract.

♦ The trial court relied on the cancellation clause to dismiss the complaint. However, the LOI included detailed terms of the agreement and stated that P had been awarded the contract for the project. The letter stated that it authorized the work, which was to commence four to 11 days after the date of the letter. These facts suggest that the parties intended to be bound so the work could begin on time.

♦ There would be no need to cancel the LOI if the parties did not intend it to be binding. A reasonable interpretation could be that the parties intended to be bound by the LOI until the formal contract was signed. Because the LOI also referred to the execution of a formal contract, it was ambiguous regarding the parties' intent. On remand, the court should submit the factual determination to the jury because the parties' intent is controlling.

Concurrence. The LOI is just ambiguous enough for P's complaint to survive a motion to dismiss. However, the most plausible interpretation of this LOI is a commitment to achieve a construction contract on the terms it contains; in other words, it is a contract to engage in negotiations.

Comment. In writing a letter of intent, a drafter should avoid ambiguity regarding the issuer's intent to be bound, and recipients should be aware that normally an LOI is not a binding contract.

---

5.   **Electronic Contracting.**

a. **Introduction.** The traditional battle of the forms took on a new dimension with the advent of electronic contracting. Consumers commonly order products over a telephone or web page with no detailed discussion of contract terms. When they receive the product, it comes with contract terms they have never seen before.

b. **Arbitration clause in consumer contract--**

Brower v. Gateway 2000, Inc., 676 N.Y.S.2d 569 (N.Y. App. Div. 1998).

Facts. Brower and other consumers (Ps) purchased computer products from Gateway 2000, Inc. (D), by mail or telephone order. D shipped Ps the merchandise accompanied by a copy of its "Standard Terms and Conditions Agreement" and associated warranties. By its terms, the agreement became binding on Ps once they kept D's merchandise more than 30 days after the date of delivery. Another term in the agreement required all disputes to be resolved by binding arbitration through the International Chamber of Commerce (ICC), with a venue in Chicago. The ICC was headquartered in France and required a deposit of $4,000 ($2,000 nonrefundable) to go to arbitration. Ps sued for damages for various complaints, but D moved to dismiss based on the arbitration clause. Ps argued that the clause was unconscionable because of the complexity of dealing with a French organization and because most of the claims against D did not exceed $1,000, which was half of the nonrefundable arbitration deposit. The court dismissed the complaint based on the arbitration clause. Ps appeal.

Issue. Where an arbitration clause in a consumer purchase agreement requires the consumer to make a nonrefundable pre-arbitration deposit that exceeds the value of the claim, is the clause unconscionable?

Held. Yes. Judgment affirmed in part, modified in part, and case remanded.

♦ Ps claim that the arbitration clause was a material alteration of a preexisting oral agreement, constituting an invalid proposal for an addition to the contract with D. However, the arbitration clause was not a material alteration of an oral agreement, but was one provision of the only contract between the parties. As held in *ProCD, Inc. v. Zeidenberg, infra*, the contract became effective once Ps kept D's merchandise beyond the 30 days specified in the agreement enclosed with the merchandise.

♦ The technique of having payment precede the revelation of the full terms of the contract is common in certain industries, such as those involving mail order. There is no contract between the parties upon placement of the order or even receiving the goods. The contract becomes binding only when the consumer keeps the product for more than 30 days.

♦ Ps also claim that the arbitration clause was a contract of adhesion, but Ps had the option to return D's product and buy a competitor's product instead. The burden of returning the merchandise is a fair trade-off for the convenience and savings of shopping by phone or mail.

♦   Ps finally claim that the arbitration clause was unconscionable. Under New York law, unconscionability usually requires a showing that the contract was both procedurally and substantively unconscionable when made. In this case, there was no procedural unconscionability because Ps had a choice as to whether to accept the contract, and the arbitration clause was not hidden in any way.

♦   However, a finding of substantive unconscionability alone may suffice. It was not unconscionable to require arbitration in Chicago. But it was unconscionable to require arbitrating before the ICC, as the excessive cost deters the individual consumer from invoking the process. Consumers give up their right to take their case to court and are left with a prohibitively expensive arbitration alternative, which in reality leaves them with no forum at all to solve disputes.

♦   On remand, the parties should have the opportunity to seek appropriate substitution of an arbitrator instead of arbitrating through the ICC.

Comment. In *ProCD, Inc. v. Zeidenberg*, 86 F.3d 1447 (7th Cir. 1996), the court held that the terms inside a box of software are binding on consumers who use the software after having an opportunity to read the terms and return the product if they disagree with the terms. The court explained that the vendor is the master of the offer and may invite acceptance by conduct. The buyer may accept by performing the specified acts. In *Hill v. Gateway 2000*, 105 F.3d 1147 (7th Cir. 1997), the court applied the *ProCD* holding to the mail order purchase of a computer system. The court found that there was no rationale to limiting *ProCD* to software and that the approve-or-return method is an efficient way to conduct commerce, whether the commerce involves software or tangible products.

1)   **Alternative to approve-or-return approach.** In *Klocek v. Gateway, Inc.*, 104 F. Supp. 2d 1332 (D. Kan. 2000), the court held that a consumer who purchases computer equipment by mail is not bound by the terms of a writing contained in the computer box where the vendor did not expressly make its acceptance of the buyer's offer to purchase contingent on the buyer's acceptance of the vendor's different or additional terms. The court asserted that in consumer transactions, the purchaser is the offeror and the vendor is the offeree. The court stated that under U.C.C. section 2-207, the seller's standard terms are either an expression of acceptance or a written confirmation. If an acceptance, the standard terms would constitute a counteroffer only if the seller expressly made its acceptance conditional on the buyer's assent to the additional or different terms.

c.   Restrictive legend on information provided--

Register.com, Inc. v. Verio, Inc., 356 F.3d 393 (2d Cir. 2004).

Facts. Register.com, Inc. (P) was one of over 50 companies that served as registrars for domain names on the Internet. P was appointed as a registrar by the Internet Corporation for Assigned Names and Numbers ("ICANN"), a private non-profit corporation. P's agreement with ICANN required P to preserve the registrant contact information, or "WHOIS" information, and to update the information daily and provide free public access to it through the Internet. Access to the WHOIS information was available only when accompanied by a legend that stated that the user would use the information for lawful purposes and would not transmit mass unsolicited email, which P later amended to include direct mail or telephone contact. P also provided web-related services that it marketed to the entities whose domain names P registered. During the registration process, P gave registrants an option to elect whether or not they wanted to receive P's marketing communications. Verio (D), who also provided web-related services in competition with P, used the WHOIS data to find new registrants and then sent those registrants marketing materials by email and other channels. P demanded that D cease using the WHOIS information for solicitation by email, direct mail, or telephone. D stopped using it for email but continued using the other channels. P sought a preliminary injunction. The district court granted a preliminary injunction as to all channels. D appeals.

Issue. Where a web-based information provider includes a restricted-use provision each time it provides information, is the provision binding on a user who obtains information daily?

Held. Yes. Judgment affirmed.

♦   D claims that it was never contractually bound to P's restrictive legend because the legend did not appear until after D had submitted the inquiry and received the WHOIS data. Thus, it had no prior notice and could not be deemed to have agreed to P's conditions.

♦   D's position might be persuasive if its inquiries were infrequent, but D made inquiries in large numbers on a daily basis. D therefore knew of P's terms. This case is distinguishable from *Specht v. Netscape Communications Corp.*, 306 F.3d 17 (2d Cir. 2002), in which the users only downloaded the software once and did not see the license unless they scrolled down their screens. The evidence in *Specht* did not show that a user who downloaded Netscape's software had necessarily seen the terms of its offer. Moreover, in this case, D admitted that it was fully aware of the terms on which P offered the access.

♦   D also claims that it was not bound by P's terms because it rejected them. Standard contract doctrine provides that when a benefit is offered subject to stated conditions, and the offeree decides to take the benefit with knowledge of the terms, the taking is an acceptance of the terms and the terms become binding. D had the choice of taking the information subject to P's terms or not taking the information at all.

Comment. Under the agreement with ICANN, P was required to permit use of the WHOIS data "for any lawful purpose except to . . . support the transmission of mass unsolicited solicitations via email (spam)." When P amended its legend to bar mass solicitation via direct mail and telephone, as well as via email, the legend no longer conformed to the agreement. D claimed that P's restrictions on the use of the WHOIS information for solicitations via direct mail or by telephone violated the ICANN agreement, but the court held that D was a third-party beneficiary that could not assert a violation of the ICANN agreement.

———————————————————

III. LIABILITY IN THE ABSENCE OF BARGAINED-FOR EXCHANGE: PROMISSORY ESTOPPEL AND RESTITUTION

A. THE DOCTRINE OF PROMISSORY ESTOPPEL

1. **Introduction.** Reliance on a promise to one's detriment may operate as a substitute for legally sufficient consideration, making a promise enforceable that otherwise would not be. This concept is known as promissory estoppel.

   a. **Traditional view.** Before the doctrine of promissory estoppel was established, the rule that agreements were not enforceable absent bargained-for consideration was rigidly enforced. One relied on promises of another at his own risk, unless one had given legal consideration for the promise.

   b. **Modern trend.** The modern trend is to enforce promises that one relies on to his detriment so long as such reliance is reasonable and foreseeable.

   c. **Gifts vs. bargain promises.** Traditionally, the doctrine of promissory estoppel had been recognized only where reliance was on a gratuitous promise, as opposed to a promise intended as a bargain but which for some reason proves to be unenforceable (*e.g.,* a promise which is too indefinite, illusory, or otherwise without consideration). If the parties were bargaining, the courts have tended to leave the parties in the position that they placed themselves in; *i.e.,* the mere fact that one party has detrimentally relied on the unenforceable promise of the other has not been enough to make the promise enforceable. However, many courts have applied the doctrine of promissory estoppel even in commercial situations—at least to the extent of allowing recovery of the expenses incurred in good-faith reliance on the promise.

2. **Requirements.** Under the original Restatement section 90, a promisor will be estopped to deny the enforceability of his promise if the following elements appear:

   a. The promisor made a promise which, although gratuitous, was the type of promise that might foreseeably induce the promisee to rely or to take some action based thereon;

   b. The promisee did in fact rely thereon, and his reliance was reasonable under the circumstances;

c.   As a result of such reliance, the promisee has suffered a substantial economic detriment; and

d.   Injustice can be avoided only by enforcing the promise.

3.   **Restatement (Second).** Under the Restatement (Second), the remedy may be limited to the extent of the reliance, rather than allowing recovery for the full promised performance.

4.   **Family Promises.** Many of the cases involving gratuitous or donative promises arise in a family context. Typically, the promise is informal and there is a dispute among family members about what was actually promised. Because no consideration is given for a gratuitous or donative promise, it is generally unenforceable. Early cases held that donative promises were unenforceable even if relied on. However, modern courts usually apply the principles of promissory estoppel in family cases.

a.   **Reliance on promise to provide home--**

Kirksey v. Kirksey, 8 Ala. 131 (1845).

Facts. Kirksey's (P's) deceased husband's brother, Kirksey (D), invited P to bring her children to his farm, promising to provide a home for P and the children on the farm until the children grew up. P moved the 70 miles to the farm with her children. After two years, D required P and the children to leave. P sued for breach of contract and won a judgment for damages in the trial court. D appeals.

Issue. Is a gratuitous promise legally enforceable after P has suffered loss and inconvenience in reliance on the promise?

Held. No. Judgment reversed.

♦   D merely gave a gift. There was no consideration to justify enforcement of the promise.

Dissent. Loss and inconvenience to P is sufficient consideration.

Comment. Promissory estoppel avoids the harsh consequences of cases like this one.

b.   **Promisee moving in reliance on promise--**

Greiner v. Greiner, 293 P. 759 (Kan. 1930).

Facts. Peter Greiner died testate, disinheriting four of his children, including Frank Greiner (D), by giving them only $5 each. Peter's widow, Maggie Greiner (P), inherited considerable property from one of her other sons. P decided to give D's brother $2,000 and give D 80 acres if he would move back and live on the property. D moved back and P moved a house from another property onto the 80 acres, where D lived for about a year before P filed the lawsuit. P eventually brought an action of forcible detention against D to recover possession. D counterclaimed, seeking title to the property. The trial court found for D. P appeals.

Issue. If a promise induces reliance by the promisee, may the promise be an enforceable contract?

Held. Yes. Judgment affirmed.

♦   Although there was conflicting testimony about P's intentions, it is clear that P promised to give D the land for the home if he would move back. P arranged to have the house moved to the property and she gave him possession of it.

♦   P claims there was no consideration for the promise, but the law recognizes that if a promise reasonably induces definite and substantial action, and the promisee does take the induced action, then the promise is binding if injustice can be avoided only by enforcement of the promise. P's promise clearly fits within this principle.

Comment. The doctrine of promissory estoppel in Restatement section 90 is commonly described as a means of protecting detrimental reliance.

---

c.   **Contract law requiring child support payments--**

Wright v. Newman, 467 S.E.2d 533 (Ga. 1996).

Facts. Wright (D) was the father of the daughter of Newman (P), but not the father of P's son. Despite that, D promised both P and her son that D would assume all the obligations of fatherhood, including providing support. D was listed on the son's birth certificate and gave the boy his last name. For 10 years, he held himself out to others as the father of the child. When D stopped supporting the children, P sued to recover child support. D proved he was not the boy's father using a DNA test. The trial court awarded P child support anyway, relying on promissory estoppel. D appeals.

Issue. Can a man who is neither the natural nor the adoptive father of a child be required to pay child support if he has promised to pay support and has held himself out as the child's father?

Held. Yes. Judgment affirmed.

- By statute, D would only be required to pay child support if he was the natural or adoptive father of the child.

- The trial court found that D allowed the child to consider D as his father, and that P had refrained from identifying and seeking support from the child's natural father as a result. If not for D's promise to support the child, P might have an alternative source of financial support for the child.

- After 10 years of honoring his voluntary commitment, D should not be allowed to evade the consequences of his promise or an injustice to P and her son would result. Under the contractual doctrine of promissory estoppel, D must be compelled to continue providing child support.

Concurrence. The doctrine of promissory estoppel prevents a promisor from reneging on a promise where the promisor knew the promisee would rely, she does in fact rely, and the reliance is to her detriment. Here, D knew P would rely on his promise. So long as the reliance is reasonable, it is sufficient to justify enforcement of the promise. There is no requirement that P must first seek to find the natural father and recover child support from him.

Dissent. There was no evidence that P could not institute a child support action against the natural father, and not even any evidence that she does not know who he is. P and D split up when the child was three years old and did not communicate again until the child was eight. D was only visiting the child for the last two years, and has not supported the child since he and P split up. P did not rely on D's promise of support for the past seven years, so detrimental reliance should not apply in this case.

---

5. **Charitable Subscriptions.**

    a. **Introduction.** A charitable subscription is an oral or written promise to give real or personal property to a charity or for a charitable purpose. In most jurisdictions, a charitable subscription must be supported by consideration or reliance to be enforceable. However, the Restatement (Second) section 90(2) provides that a charitable subscription is binding without proof that the promise induced action or forbearance.

    b. **Recipient's reliance on charitable subscription--**

King v. Trustees of Boston University, 647 N.E.2d 1196 (Mass. 1995).

Facts. Dr. Martin Luther King, Jr., deposited some of his papers with the Trustees of Boston University (D). Around the same time, King was approached by other universities seeking his papers. King wrote a letter to D naming D as the repository of the papers in which he stated that the papers would remain his legal property, but he also expressed his intention to give the papers to D as an outright gift, and in the event of his death, the papers would become D's property. King's administratrix, Coretta Scott King (P), sued D for conversion, claiming that D did not hold title to the papers. The jury found that D had acquired rightful ownership of the papers through a charitable pledge, but not a contract. The trial court denied P's motion for judgment n.o.v. or a new trial. P appeals.

Issue. If there is evidence of a donative intent, may a charitable subscription become enforceable if the recipient of the property spends money to care for the property?

Held. Yes. Judgment affirmed.

◆ The letter D relies on includes an intention to donate the papers gradually over time and an intention to leave all the papers to D in the event of death. When construing charitable subscriptions, the objective is to give effect to clear donative intent to the extent possible without abandoning basic contractual principles.

◆ The fact that Dr. King established a bailment with D by delivering the papers to D could be viewed by the jury as security for the promise to give the papers in the future. This supports a finding that Dr. King had donative intent. The statement of transfer to take place upon his death was not a will, but a contract or promise to take effect at his death.

◆ As for evidence of consideration or reliance, D indexed the papers, made them available to researchers, and provided trained staff to care for them. D held a convocation to commemorate receipt of the papers, and Dr. King spoke at the convocation. The jury could reasonably conclude that these activities exceeded what would be expected of a mere bailee and constituted reliance or consideration for Dr. King's promises.

---

6. **Commercial Contracts.**

    a. **Introduction.** The early cases involving promissory estoppel involved noncommercial situations, with the exception of employee benefit or pension cases such as *Plowman, supra.* Eventually, the doctrine extended to commercial promises that lacked consideration.

    b. **Promise inducing retirement--**

Katz v. Danny Dare, Inc., 610 S.W.2d 121 (Mo. Ct. App. 1980).

Facts. Katz (P) worked for Danny Dare, Inc. (D) for 25 years. After 23 years, P was injured when trying to prevent a theft from one of D's stores. P became somewhat incapacitated as a result, and D wanted to induce P to retire. P did not want to retire, but after months of negotiations, P accepted a pension offer from D for $13,000 per year for life. Subsequently, P began working for D again on a part-time basis. D stopped sending the checks to P on the ground that P had recovered enough to work. P sued. The trial court found for D on the grounds that P did not give up anything to which he was legally entitled when he decided to retire; *i.e.*, he had the choice of retiring with a pension or being fired. P appeals.

Issue. If an at-will employee accepts an offer for a retirement pension, may his reliance support a claim of promissory estoppel even if the employer could have fired him instead of offering the retirement pension?

Held. Yes. Judgment reversed.

♦ P relies on *Feinberg v. Pfeiffer Co.*, 322 S.W.2d 163 (Mo. Ct. App. 1959), in which the court applied promissory estoppel to a pension case, following the example in Restatement section 90. D claims that because P's alternative was getting fired, the case falls outside *Feinberg*.

♦ D's threat to fire P if he did not retire does not take the case outside of *Feinberg*. P was not actually fired; instead, D negotiated with P for several months before P accepted the retirement offer. D's board of directors adopted a resolution promising to pay P the pension. By so doing, he gave up $10,000 a year in earnings that he would have made had he continued working for D.

♦ The trial court improperly required P to show that he gave up something to which he was legally entitled before he could enforce the pension promise. Instead, P's reliance on D's promise is sufficient, combined with the fact that injustice can be avoided only by enforcement of D's promise.

---

c.   **Promise inducing promisee not to act--**

Shoemaker v. Commonwealth Bank, 700 A.2d 1003 (Pa. Super. Ct. 1997).

Facts. The Shoemakers (Ps) got a $25,000 mortgage on their home from Commonwealth Bank (D). The mortgage agreement required Ps to carry insurance on the property, but they allowed the insurance to expire in 1994. In 1995, Ps' house was destroyed by fire. Ps claim that in 1994, D sent them a notice that their insurance had been cancelled and that if they did not purchase a new policy, D might be forced to purchase insurance and add it to Ps' loan balance. A representative of D also telephoned Ps and told them the same thing. Ps claim that, based on these contacts, they assumed D had obtained the insurance. Only after the house burned did Ps discover the house was uninsured. D did actually get insurance for 1994, but it expired in December 1994. D claims that it sent a letter to Ps informing them of this expiration and reminding them to get insurance. Ps denied having received the letter. Ps sued D for promissory estoppel, breach of contract, and fraud. D moved for summary judgment. The court granted the motion on the ground that D had actually obtained the insurance, even if it had subsequently expired. Ps appeal.

Issue. May a mortgagor who is required to carry property insurance recover in promissory estoppel from the mortgagee who made an oral promise to obtain insurance but failed to do so?

Held. Yes. Judgment reversed in part.

- ♦ Ps' fraud claim was properly dismissed because the breach of a promise to do something in the future is not actionable in fraud.

- ♦ Ps' promissory estoppel claim requires proof that D made a promise it reasonably expected would induce forbearance on the part of Ps; that Ps actually refrained from taking action in reliance on the promise; and that injustice can be avoided only by enforcing the promise.

- ♦ Ps claim that D promised to get insurance and charge Ps for the cost of the premium. Other courts have considered this issue and concluded that such a promise is actionable. Ps' obligation to carry insurance does not prevent them from contracting with someone else to obtain the insurance for them.

- ♦ Ps have offered evidence sufficient to allow a jury to find that D made a promise that Ps relied on, and that injustice could be avoided only by enforcing that promise. The court should not have granted D's motion for summary judgment.

B. THE PRINCIPLE OF RESTITUTION

1. **Restitution Without a Promise.** Even when there is no expression of assent by a party, either by words or deeds, a contract may be imposed by law under the doctrine of contract implied in law. Such a contract is based on a legal fiction that arises from considerations of justice and equitable principles of unjust enrichment. Restitution and unjust enrichment are modern terms for what used to be called quasi contracts or contracts implied in law.

    a. **Unwanted medical services provided to mentally incompetent patient--**

Credit Bureau Enterprises, Inc. v. Pelo, 608 N.W.2d 20 (Iowa 2000).

Facts. Pelo (D) threatened to hurt himself, and the police took him to the hospital. A magistrate entered an emergency hospitalization order, requiring D to be detained for 48 hours. D refused to sign a release form, but later relented to protect his personal items. The form provided that D was liable for any charges not covered by insurance. After D was released, the hospital sought payment of a bill for $2,775. D refused to pay the bill or authorize his insurance carrier to pay it. The hospital assigned its claim to Credit Bureau Enterprises, Inc. (P). P sued in small claims court. At a hearing on the claim, D admitted he was hospitalized, but denied making any agreement to pay for the services. He claimed he had signed the consent form under duress. The court awarded judgment to P. D appealed. The district court affirmed, concluding that the release form was a valid, enforceable contract, and, in the alternative, D was liable under a theory of implied contract. The Iowa Supreme Court granted review.

Issue. May a hospital patient be required to pay for medical services he receives, even if he did not consent to the services, did not want them, and was mentally incompetent at the time?

Held. Yes. Judgment affirmed.

♦ Under the principles of unjust enrichment, a person who benefits from the acts of another may be required to make restitution to the actor, where the person performs services that the recipient knows about and accepts. It is generally accepted that a patient is liable for the reasonable value of medical services rendered by a hospital.

♦ The law does not normally permit restitution where the benefit is forced upon the recipient against his will. There are circumstances in which an unwanted service can be the basis for restitution. One of these circumstances is where it was impossible for the recipient to give consent or where, because of mental impairment, the recipient's consent would have been immaterial.

♦ The factual basis for D's hospitalization is not in dispute. Nor is D's diagnosis as suffering bipolar disorder, a mental illness. D claims he should not have to pay because he did not ask to be hospitalized, because he derived no benefit from the hospitalization, and because the referee's determination that further hospitalization was not authorized showed that he should not have been hospitalized in the first place. However, the referee's determination only pertained to future hospitalization. D's opinion as to the initial need for hospitalization is irrelevant because that need was established by the magistrate.

♦ Finally, D did derive medical benefit from the hospitalization. If nothing else, the reports of the physicians regarding D's need for further treatment were a benefit to D. All the requirements of an implied contract in law were satisfied, and D is liable.

Comment. The court did not address the issue of whether D's signing of the consent form constituted an express contract, because they decided he was liable under the quasi contract theory.

---

b. **Subcontractor claims under quasi contract--**

Commerce Partnership 8098 Limited Partnership v. Equity Contracting Co., 695 So. 2d 383 (Fl. Dist. Ct. App. 1997).

Facts. Equity Contracting Co. (P) was a stucco subcontractor on a project to improve an office building owned by Commerce Partnership 8098 Limited Partnership (D). P performed the work but was not paid by the general contractor. P refused to do remedial work requested by D after an inspection unless D paid P at least part of the amount due. P sued the general contractor, who later declared bankruptcy. P sued D for the reasonable value of the work, which was $17,100. After P rested, D moved for dismissal on the ground that the evidence did not support a contract implied in fact. The trial court denied the motion. During closing argument, P's lawyer stated it had made a claim for quantum meruit. The trial court agreed that this was the first time that issue had been raised, so he allowed D to reopen his case. D claimed that it had paid the general contractor in full, although the total of its payments were less than the total contract price. The court declined to allow evidence that D had paid other subcontractors $64,000 directly on the ground that it was irrelevant. The trial court granted judgment to P for $17,100. D appeals.

Issue. May a subcontractor who has not been paid for work done because the general contractor has gone bankrupt recover in quasi contract from the owner of the building that the subcontractor worked on, if the owner paid the general contractor for the work done by the subcontractor?

Held. No. Judgment reversed and case remanded.

♦   There was confusion at trial about the differences between a contract implied in fact and a contract implied in law. The confusion arises because a contract implied in law has been referred to with several terms, including "quasi contract," "unjust enrichment," "restitution," "constructive contract," and "quantum meruit." The preferred term is "quasi contract."

♦   A contract implied in fact is an enforceable contract based on a tacit promise inferred in whole or in part from the parties' conduct. This must arise from the interaction of the parties or their agents.

♦   A contract implied in law, also called a quasi contract, is not based on an agreement between the parties but on an obligation created by the law without regard to the parties' expression of assent. The parties may not even have had any dealings with each other. It is essentially a remedy provided for one who confers a benefit without receiving compensation. The elements of a quasi contract cause of action are: (i) a benefit conferred by P upon D; (ii) D has knowledge of the benefit; (iii) D has accepted or retained the benefit; and (iv) the circumstances are such that it would be inequitable for D to retain the benefit without paying fair value for it.

♦   Some cases can involve both contracts implied in fact and quasi contract. In this case, P was making a quasi contract claim, not a claim based on contract implied in fact.

♦   To prevail in a claim based on quasi contract, a subcontractor must establish that (i) it has exhausted all remedies against the general contractor and still remained unpaid, and (ii) the owner had not paid any other person for the improvements furnished by the subcontractor. These requirements make sure that the enrichment of the owner is truly unjust when compared to the uncompensated subcontractor.

♦   In this case, D claims it paid more than the contract price, since it paid the $64,000 to other subcontractors. The trial court erred in not admitting this evidence. On remand, P has the burden to show that D did not pay anyone else for the work done by P. If P can do so, the court should enter judgment for P. If P cannot prove that D did not pay for that work, then it should enter judgment for D.

─────────────

c.   **Property division in unmarried cohabitation--**

Watts v. Watts, 405 N.W.2d 303 (Wis. 1987).

Facts. Sue Ann Watts (P) and James Watts (D) moved in together and began living as husband and wife, but they never married. P assumed D's surname as her own. P and D had two children, filed joint income tax returns, and held joint bank accounts. They purchased property as husband and wife. P contributed childcare and homemaking services, as well as personal property. P occasionally worked at D's office and started a business with D's sister-in-law. Eventually, P left the home in response to D's behavior. P filed suit for an accounting of the property P and D acquired together because D refused to share it or to compensate P for her contributions to the relationship. The trial court dismissed P's complaint for failure to state a claim upon which relief may be granted, concluding that the statutory provisions for division of property only applied to married couples. P appeals.

Issue. May the courts divide property between persons who have engaged in nonmarital cohabitation, where the property division statute applies to married persons only?

Held. Yes. Judgment reversed.

- The trial court properly rejected P's claim under the property division statute because it expressly applies to married couples and was not intended to extend to unmarried cohabitants. P also claims that D should be estopped from asserting the lack of a legal marriage as a defense to her statutory claim, but the doctrine of "marriage by estoppel" should not apply here because the statute requires actual marriage.

- P claims that she and D had a contract to share equally the property they accumulated during their relationship. In a prior case, *Hewitt v. Hewitt*, 394 N.E.2d 1204 (Ill. 1979), the court held that judicial recognition of mutual property rights between unmarried cohabitants would violate the public policy of the Illinois Marriage Act because it would make unmarried cohabitation more attractive. *Hewitt* has been criticized and its holding is inconsistent with the principle that requires narrow application of public policy limits. Besides, Illinois law provides for "fault" divorce, while Wisconsin has abolished both "fault" divorce and criminal sanctions against nonmarital cohabitation.

- D asserts that only the legislature can specify the rules regarding property division for cohabiting parties. While the legislature could enter this arena, the courts need not refrain from considering contract and property law questions involving unmarried cohabitants.

- D also claims that because his relationship with P was immoral and illegal, any contract based on that relationship would contravene public policy. The rule in this situation is that so long as the contract is independent of the illicit relationship and the illicit relationship is not any part of the consideration bargained for, the contract may be enforceable. The alternative is to deprive one party of the property she helped accumulate.

- P has alleged sufficient facts to state a claim for damages resulting from D's breach of an express or implied in fact contract to share all the property accumulated through the efforts of both parties during their relationship.

- P has also stated a claim for unjust enrichment or quasi contract. She has alleged that she conferred a benefit on D, that D knew of the benefit, and that D accepted the benefit under circumstances making it inequitable for D to retain the benefit. If proven, these allegations would satisfy the requirements for an unjust enrichment claim.

---

2. **Promissory Restitution.** As discussed *supra*, the traditional rule does not enforce a promise for benefits previously received on the ground that such benefits are past consideration. The modern trend is to enforce a promise

based on a moral obligation if the promise is based on an economic benefit previously given to the promisor and enforcement is necessary to prevent injustice.

a. Traditional approach denying enforcement--

Mills v. Wyman, 20 Mass. (3 Pick.) 207 (1825).

Facts. Mills (P) took in Wyman's (D's) 25-year-old son who was poor and had become sick on a sea voyage. P cared for him for two weeks. D subsequently promised to repay P's expenses, but then changed his mind. P sued to recover the expenses. The court granted nonsuit to D. P appeals.

Issue. Does a moral obligation constitute sufficient consideration to make a promise enforceable?

Held. No. Judgment affirmed.

♦ A moral obligation is generally not sufficient consideration for an express promise. The execution of such a promise is left to the conscience of the promisor.

♦ The law will only give a promise validity if the promisor gains something, or the promisee loses something, by the promise.

b. Modern approach allowing enforcement--

Webb v. McGowin, 168 So. 196 (Ala. Ct. App. 1935), *cert. denied*, 168 So. 199 (Ala. 1936).

Facts. Webb (P) was cleaning the upper floor of a mill and was about to drop a heavy weight to the floor below. P saw McGowin there, and in the process of avoiding harm to him, P himself fell and sustained permanent injuries. McGowin promised to pay P a monthly sum for life, and made payments for eight years until he died. McGowin's executor (D) stopped the payments. P sued. D was granted a nonsuit. P appeals.

Issue. Is moral consideration sufficient to support a promise given in recognition of a past economic benefit received by the promisor?

Held. Yes. Judgment reversed.

♦ Where the promisor receives a material benefit, and the promisee suffers a material detriment, moral obligation is sufficient consideration to support a promise.

♦ In this case, McGowin received a material benefit of not being injured, and P suffered a material detriment of permanent disability.

Comment. Note that even when the only consideration is moral obligation, the courts may enforce the contract if the promisee has detrimentally relied on the promise.

———

IV. THE STATUTE OF FRAUDS

A. INTRODUCTION

1. **History.** In most instances, oral contracts are valid. However, by statute, a few types of contracts are required to be in writing, or at least evidenced by a signed, written memorandum of the essential terms. These statutory requirements stem from the English Statute of Frauds of 1677.

2. **Purpose.** The purpose of the Statute of Frauds is to prevent fraud and perjury as to the actual terms of the contract and to provide better evidence of the contract terms in the event of dispute. Failure to comply with the Statute renders the contract voidable but not void. Thus, the Statute relates only to the remedy and not to the substantive validity of the contract.

3. **Types of Contracts Covered.** The Statute of Frauds requires a writing for contracts that cannot be enforced within one year, for a guarantee of another's debts, and for contracts involving an interest in land, including leases.

B. TYPES OF CONTRACTS THAT MUST BE IN WRITING

1. **Contracts that Cannot Be Performed Within One Year.**

   a. **General rule.** Contracts that by their terms cannot by any possibility be performed within one year from the date the contract is made must be in writing.

   b. **Exceptions.**

      1) **Performance within one year possible.** Some contracts that seem to envision performance over longer than one year are nonetheless capable of being fully performed within one year, even though it is highly unlikely that they will be performed within that period of time. Such contracts are not within the Statute, and hence are enforceable although oral.

         a) **Performance on happening of condition.** An oral agreement to perform on a condition that conceivably might occur within one year is not subject to the Statute of Frauds—regardless of how unlikely it is that the condition will occur within that time.

         b) **Performance until happening of condition.** Likewise, contracts to perform until the happening of some condition that conceivably might occur within one year are enforceable, although oral.

      c)   **Alternative performance possible within year.** Agreements for alternative performances, any one of which is capable of full performance within one year (*e.g.*, to furnish goods to another "for five years, or as long as he should remain in business"), are enforceable, although oral.

   2)   **Fully executed contracts.** Even if a contract is impossible to perform within one year, the great weight of authority holds that if it is fully executed on one side, this will take the entire contract out of the Statute and make the oral promise enforceable. This avoids the injustice that would result if the party who had received the other's performance could use the Statute to escape his own obligations.

  c.   **Contracts to make a will, or to be performed after death.** In some states, the Statute of Frauds requiring contracts incapable of performance within one year to be in writing is extended to contracts not to be performed during the lifetime of the promisor, as well as to agreements to make a will or devise or bequeath property.

2.   **Other Contracts Within the Statute.**

  a.   **Guarantee contracts.** Promises to answer for or discharge the debts of another must be in writing to be enforceable. This applies only to promises made (i) by one who is not currently liable for the debt, (ii) to a creditor, and (iii) in order to discharge the present or future obligations of a third person.

   1)   **Promises to debtor.** If the promise is made to the debtor ("I'll pay your obligation to X") and is supported by consideration, it is enforceable even though it is oral. [*See* Restatement (Second) §112] Novations are not within the Statute of Frauds, either. [*See* Restatement (Second) §115]

   2)   **Primary debt by promisor.** The Statute does not apply to "primary promises." This means that if the underlying contract was between the promisor and the creditor, the promise is enforceable, although oral. [*See* Restatement (Second) §114] Thus, if A orally tells C to send $100 of goods to B and "send the bill for $100 to me," the primary contract is between A and C. B is merely a third-party beneficiary, and the contract is enforceable.

   3)   **Exception—guarantor's main purpose is to benefit himself.** Even if the promise is "collateral," if it appears that the promisor's main purpose in guaranteeing the obligation of another was to secure an advantage or pecuniary benefit for himself, his promise is enforceable even though not in writing. [*See* Restatement (Second) §116]

b. **Contracts in consideration of marriage.** The marriage provision in the Statute of Frauds refers to marriage settlement contracts or premarriage contracts. The Statute of Frauds does not apply to mutual promises to marry between prospective spouses.

c. **Contracts for the sale of an interest in land.** A contract for the sale of land or any interest therein must be in writing.

   1) **Leases.** Leases are normally covered by the Statute of Frauds; however, many states provide by statute that only leases for more than a year have to be in writing.

   2) **An "interest" in land.** It is often difficult to determine what is included under the term "interest in land." Fixtures, liens, growing timber, etc., all have been held to be "interests" in land.

3. **The Required Writing.** To qualify as a writing, the document must be in a permanent, written form and signed by the party to be charged. It need not be a fully integrated, formal contract, however.

   a. **Memorandum of essential terms.** A memorandum of the essential terms of the agreement (*e.g.*, letters, telegrams, or even mere notations in the private books of one of the parties that were never communicated to the other) may satisfy the Statute. The memorandum must contain the following elements:

      1) Identity of the contracting parties;

      2) Description of the subject matter of the contract;

      3) Terms and conditions of the agreement;

      4) Recital of the consideration; and

      5) Signature of the party to be charged. The party's initials or seal may be sufficient.

   b. **Integration of documents.** The requisite writing may be composed of several documents, provided each document refers to or incorporates the others, or they are otherwise integrated (*i.e.*, are physically attached).

      1) **Integration of several writings--**

Crabtree v. Elizabeth Arden Sales Corp., 110 N.E.2d 551 (N.Y. 1953).

Facts. Crabtree (P) agreed to become sales manager for Elizabeth Arden Sales Corp. (D), and an unsigned office memorandum was prepared that set forth P's name, his starting salary of $20,000, a six-month increase to $25,000, a one-year increase to $30,000, and a notation "two years to make good." On commencement, a payroll card was prepared indicating a starting salary of $20,000 and was initialed by D's general manager. P received his scheduled increase at six months. At one year, a payroll change card was prepared and signed by D's comptroller, but Miss Arden refused to approve it. P then quit and brought suit for breach by D. From a judgment for P, D appeals.

Issue. May oral testimony be used to establish the connection between written documents to derive the terms of a contract?

Held. Yes. Judgment affirmed.

♦   The unsigned office memorandum, the payroll change card initialed by the general manager, and the payroll change card prepared and signed by the comptroller all refer to the same transaction and constitute sufficient memoranda, when taken together, to bind D.

♦   Without the unsigned memorandum, the duration of the agreement would have been in question, since neither of the payroll cards set forth the term. Thus, it was necessary for the three writings to be integrated for P to recover the $14,000 awarded by the trial court.

_____

4.   **General Exceptions to the Statute of Frauds.**

a.   **Part performance.** Part performance of an oral contract for the sale of land can make the agreement enforceable despite the Statute. A seller who conveys an interest to the buyer can recover the purchase price even if the contract was not in writing. A buyer who makes a valuable improvement on the land or who took possession and paid part of the purchase price may obtain specific performance but generally cannot sue for damages.

b.   **Reliance.** Traditionally, reliance on a contract that was within the Statute of Frauds did not create an exception to the Statute, except if it was part performance. There is a trend toward treating reliance as a form of estoppel; *i.e.*, one party's reliance on an oral contract may estop the other from asserting the Statute as a defense. The Restatement (Second) section 139 adopts this approach as necessary to avoid injustice.

c.   **Contract-related rights outside the statute--**

Winternitz v. Summit Hills Joint Venture, 532 A.2d 1089 (Md. Ct. Spec. App. 1987), *cert. denied*, 538 A.2d 778 (Md. 1988).

Facts. Winternitz (P) leased space from Summit Hills Joint Venture (D) for a pharmacy and convenience store. The lease term of six years expired January 31, 1983. In October 1982, P met with D's agent to discuss renewing the lease and selling his pharmacy. D's agent agreed to renew the lease and agreed to the assignment. In mid-January 1983, D gave P a written two-year lease with options to renew for eight more years. Neither party signed the lease, but P began paying the higher rent specified in the lease. P sold the business to the Suhs for $70,000, contingent on P getting the lease finalized. In February, D assured P that everything was okay with the lease, but in late February, D told P that it was going to negotiate its own lease and would not renew P's lease or allow P to transfer it. D gave P a 30-day eviction notice. P renegotiated the sale for a price of $15,000 and vacated the premises. P sued for breach of contract. The jury awarded P $45,000, but the judge entered a judgment n.o.v., relying on the Statute of Frauds. P appeals.

Issue. When a party breaches a contract that is unenforceable under the Statute of Frauds, may the other party still state a claim for malicious interference with contractual relationships with third parties?

Held. Yes. Judgment reversed.

♦   The Statute of Frauds applies because a leasehold cannot be granted unless in writing and signed by the grantor. Here, there was no signature on the lease.

♦   P relies on the part performance doctrine, which allows a contract for the sale of land to be specifically enforced, despite noncompliance with the Statute of Frauds, if P reasonably relied on the contract and so changed his position that injustice can be avoided only by specific enforcement. The question is whether P's part performance is sufficient evidence of an oral agreement to justify excusing compliance with the Statute of Frauds.

♦   P claims that paying the higher rental of $1,700 in February is part performance, but that issue is irrelevant in that case. Part performance is an equitable notion that does not bar application of the Statute of Frauds where P has sought only money damages and not any equitable relief.

♦   P also claims that D intentionally and maliciously interfered with P's existing contract with the Suhs. The jury found that D had agreed to renew the lease and allow P to assign it to the Suhs, that D then breached the agreement, and that D's action was taken maliciously and with the intent to injure P. D would not give P a lease because D wanted P to move out so D could negotiate its own lease.

♦   The tort of intentional interference with contractual relations allows recovery of foreseeable damages. Although the lease renewal agreement was not entirely valid under the Statute of Frauds, D was not entitled to breach it with the intent of sabotaging P's contract with the Suhs. P cannot recover for the breach of the unenforceable contract, but can recover for D's intentional interference with P's contract with the Suhs.

♦ The trial court should not have nullified the jury's verdict.

---

d. **Promissory estoppel--**

Alaska Democratic Party v. Rice, 934 P.2d 1313 (Alaska 1997).

Facts. Rice (P) was offered a two-year position with the Alaska Democratic Party (D), with a salary of $36,000 per year. P orally accepted the offer, quit her job, and moved to Alaska. P never received a written contract. A few months later, D decided not to hire P. P sued. The jury awarded P $28,864 for promissory estoppel and $1,558 for misrepresentation. The trial court disallowed the misrepresentation award to avoid a double recovery. D appeals.

Issue. May promissory estoppel be used to enforce an oral contract that falls within the Statute of Frauds?

Held. Yes. Judgment affirmed.

♦ The Statute of Frauds is intended to prevent fraud, but it cannot be used as an "escape route" for avoiding obligations. If the requirements of promissory estoppel are met, the promise can be enforced when injustice can only be avoided by enforcement of the promise, even if the contract falls within the Statute of Frauds.

♦ Allowing promissory estoppel claims in this type of case does not undermine the principle behind the Statute of Frauds, because the existence of the promise must be established by clear and convincing evidence.

Comment. Although some courts disagree with this rule, it is the rule of section 139 of the Restatement (Second) of Contracts.

C. STATUTE OF FRAUDS IN THE U.C.C.

1. **Introduction.** Under the U.C.C., a contract for the sale of goods for the price of $500 or more must be in writing. [*See* U.C.C. §2-201] Note that the floor price above which a writing is required exceeds $500 in several jurisdictions.

a. **Goods defined.** "Goods" includes all tangible movable property. It does not include intangibles, securities, or labor and services.

   1) Often a contract requires that goods be supplied as part of rendering services. The issue is whether the contract is primarily for the sale of goods or for the rendering of services.

   2) An oral contract for the service of constructing a building might be primarily for services and, even though materials worth $500 or more are supplied as part of the job, an oral contract would be enforceable.

b. **Exceptions.** Oral contracts for the sale of goods of $500 or more will be enforced in the following situations:

   1) The buyer receives and accepts all or part of the goods (the contract is enforceable as to the goods accepted);

   2) The buyer gives something in part payment for the goods (the contract is enforceable as to the goods paid for);

   3) The contract calls for the manufacture of special goods for the buyer and the seller has made a substantial beginning in the manufacture thereof;

   4) The contract is between merchants and within a reasonable time a written confirmation is sent and the party receiving it does not send a written objection within 10 days;

   5) The contract is admitted to by the party against whom enforcement is sought (in court pleadings or testimony).

c. **Related provisions.** The U.C.C. also has separate provisions that require a written contract for transactions involving "intangibles" and "securities."

2. **Part Performance by Acceptance of Check--**

Buffaloe v. Hart, 441 S.E.2d 172 (N.C. Ct. App. 1994).

Facts. Buffaloe (P), a tobacco farmer, rented five barns from the Harts (Ds) under an oral agreement. P wanted to buy the barns and offered to pay $20,000 for them, at the rate of $5,000 per year for four years. Ds accepted the offer. Ds continued paying for insurance on the barns, but P reimbursed them. P then decided to sell the barns. He sold them for $8,000 each. P made the first $5,000 payment to Ds by check. The next day, Ds told P they did not want P to sell the barns because they had already sold them. Ds returned P's check after tearing it up. Ds had sold the five barns to P's buyers. P sued. The jury found that the parties had a contract and that Ds accepted a payment for the barns. The jury awarded P $21,000. Ds appeal.

Issue. Is a personal check signed by the buyer, describing the property purchased and containing an amount representing the agreed partial payment, sufficient to constitute a writing under the Statute of Frauds?

Held. No. Judgment affirmed on other grounds.

♦ Under U.C.C. section 2-201(1), a check may satisfy the writing requirement so long as it is signed by the party against whom enforcement is sought. Ds here did not endorse the check, so their handwriting does not appear anywhere on the check. This leaves the alleged oral contract unenforceable under U.C.C. §2-201(1).

♦ Ds claim that the part performance exception of U.C.C. section 2-201(3)(c) does not apply because P took no overt action different from the rental relationship and because P's delivery of the check was not partial payment since Ds never accepted it.

♦ To constitute part performance, P must have delivered something that Ds accepted. The jury found that P did deliver the $5,000 check and that Ds did not return it for four days. This constitutes acceptance by Ds. That, combined with P's acceptance of the barns, suffices to establish that the parties had a contract.

---

3. **Merchant Confirmation Exeption.** Under U.C.C. 2-201(2), between merchants, a confirmatory writing, such as a buyer's purchase order, may create a contract.

V. THE MEANING OF THE AGREEMENT: PRINCIPLES OF INTERPRETATION AND THE PAROL EVIDENCE RULE

A. PRINCIPLES OF INTERPRETATION

1. **Introduction.** The subject of ambiguity is related to that of mistake. Ambiguity issues arise where the parties' expressions are susceptible to more than one interpretation, and thus there is uncertainty as to the meaning of the expressions.

2. **Types of Ambiguity.**

   a. **Latent ambiguity.** Although the terms may appear certain, extrinsic facts make more than one interpretation possible. The ambiguity is not apparent from the language itself.

   b. **Patent ambiguity.** This arises when the uncertainty is obvious from the words used. Example: A agrees to sell "my property" to B. Because the uncertainty is too great, there is no contract.

3. **Rules Governing Latent Ambiguity Problems.**

   a. **Where both parties are unaware of the ambiguity.** This is like a mutual mistake concerning a material fact. Because each party has a reasonable interpretation, and neither party knows of the other's interpretation or has reason to know of it, there is no contract.

   b. **Where both parties are aware.** If both parties are aware of the ambiguity, then there is a contract only if they both agree on the same interpretation.

   c. **Where only one party knows.** If one party knows or has reason to know that the words used are ambiguous, but the other party does not know, then there is a binding contract according to the interpretation of the innocent party.

4. **Importance of Determining What the Parties Know--**

Joyner v. Adams, 361 S.E.2d 902 (N.C. Ct. App. 1987).

Facts. Joyner (P) owned real property that she wanted to develop. P contracted with Brown to develop the property. Brown entered a "Base Lease" for the entire property, with a rent escalation clause based on the Wholesale Price Index. Brown would prepare the land and then subdivide it into individual lots, for which individual "Lot Leases" would replace the "Base Lease." In 1975, the parties substituted Adams (D) for Brown and suspended the annual rent increases until September 1980, at which point D was to have subdivided all the land so that every lot is "eligible for the execution" of a Lot Lease. If D failed to do so, he was obligated to pay the rent increases under the Base Lease retroactively. By the end of September, D had executed lot leases for every lot but one, and that one was graded and prepared for building, but did not have a building on it. P sued, claiming D had failed to fully develop the property. The trial court granted summary judgment for D, but the court of appeals reversed. On remand, the trial court found that there had been no meeting of the minds regarding the meaning of what development was required, but that since D had drafted the amended lease, it should be construed against him. The court awarded P $93,695.75. D appeals.

Issue. Where there is no meeting of the minds regarding a contract provision, must a court determine whether either party knew or had reason to know of the other's meaning of the disputed language?

Held. Yes. Judgment reversed and case remanded.

♦   As the trial court observed, there is conflicting evidence regarding the parties' intent, based on their actions and various memoranda. D intended the provision to require what D actually did; *i.e.*, develop the property to be ready for construction of a building. P clearly had a different intention. There was no meeting of the minds between these parties.

♦   When there is no meeting of the minds, but one party knows or has reason to know what the other party means and the other party does not know or have reason to know, the court enforces the contract in accordance with the innocent party's meaning. The trial court did not make findings of fact on this issue, so the case must be remanded.

♦   The trial court erred in applying the rule that ambiguity must be construed most strongly against the party who drafted the contract. That rule is appropriate in the context of an adhesion contract or where the parties had disparate bargaining positions. In this case, both P and D were experienced in the real estate business and they had equal bargaining power.

Comment. On remand, the trial court found that D did not know, or have reason to know, what P's meaning was, so it found for D. This ruling was upheld on appeal.

5.   **Subjective Meaning of Contract Term--**

Frigaliment Importing Co. v. B.N.S. International Sales Corp., 190 F. Supp. 116 (S.D.N.Y. 1960).

Facts. B.N.S. International Sales Corp. (D) contracted to sell "chicken" to Frigaliment Importing Co. (P). D shipped stewing chicken ("fowl") under both contracts instead of the broiling and frying chicken desired by P. P sues for breach of warranty.

Issue. To enforce a particular meaning of a common term used in a contract, must P prove either D's actual knowledge of the particular meaning or a widespread, universal usage in the particular manner asserted?

Held. Yes. Judgment for D.

♦ The making of a contract depends not on the agreement of two minds on one intention, but on the agreement of two sets of external signs. What the parties said, not what they meant, is the essence of the contract.

♦ P produces substantial evidence that its narrow usage of the word "chicken" is common. D, however, shows that it is relatively new in the business, did not know of this trade usage, and that in fact "chicken" is commonly used in the trade in its broadest sense, covering broilers, fryers, and stewing chickens.

♦ Furthermore, D shows that by comparing the market price and the contract price, D would have incurred a loss by shipping broilers. Thus, D believed it could properly send "fowl." P believed it would receive broilers, but P failed to meet its burden of proving that the term "chicken" was to be used in the narrower rather than in the broader sense.

Comment. This case points out the difference between having a contract term that refers equally to two different objects, and a term that has both a general and a specific trade usage, such as "chicken." [*Compare* Restatement (Second) §§200 and 201]

---

6.   Adhesion Contracts--

C & J Fertilizer, Inc. v. Allied Mutual Insurance Co., 227 N.W.2d 169 (Iowa 1975).

Facts. C & J Fertilizer, Inc. (P) was insured against burglary under policies issued by Allied Mutual Insurance Co. (D). The policies' definition of "burglary" required the exterior of the premises to bear visible marks of force and violence. P's warehouse was burglarized, but the only damage occurred to an interior door. P sued to recover for the burglary losses, but the trial court found for D. P appeals.

Issue. Will the terms of an adhesion contract be strictly enforced if the result would be forfeiture?

Held. No. Judgment reversed and case remanded.

♦ Construction of contract terms is a matter of law.

♦ When construing an adhesion contract, courts should look beyond unfair provisions that were never truly assented to and enforce the reasonable expectations of the parties.

♦ D breached an implied warranty that the writing would not alter or impair the fair meaning of the protection bargained for. D used the definition as an exclusion of coverage for which the parties clearly bargained.

♦ The liability-avoiding provision was unconscionable in these circumstances and therefore could not bar P's claim.

Dissent. The generalizations made by the majority appear proper but are inapplicable to this case because P knew exactly what the policy covered. D's exclusion was intended to deny coverage for "inside jobs," meaning those resulting from the insured's complicity.

B. THE PAROL EVIDENCE RULE

1. **Introduction.** When an agreement has been reduced to a writing that the parties intend as the final and complete expression of their agreement, evidence of any earlier oral or written expressions, or of any contemporaneous written expressions, is *not admissible* to vary, add to, or contradict the terms of the writing. Such evidence is termed *"parol evidence."*

   a. **Rationale.** The law favors written agreements over oral agreements because of the reduced opportunity for fraud, perjury, or simple error. A final, integrated written contract is more reliable evidence of the parties' intent than are tentative, preliminary expressions.

   b. **Procedural and substantive aspects.** The rule has both a procedural and substantive aspect. It operates as a rule of evidence to exclude parol evidence at trial, and as a rule of substantive contract law, setting bounds on what constitutes the contract between the parties.

2. **Determining Whether a Written Contract Is a Final and Complete Expression.** The parol evidence rule only applies if the parties intended the writing to be a final expression of their agreement. Two tests are used to determine whether it is an *"integration."*

a. **Face of the agreement test.** The old view was that the parties' intent must be determined from the face of the agreement itself. Thus, if the written agreement appeared to be complete and final, no parol evidence could be admitted.

b. **Warranty not in written contract--**

Thompson v. Libby, 26 N.W. 1 (Minn. 1885).

Facts. Thompson (P) owned logs that were lying in the river. Libby (D) agreed to purchase the logs in a written contract that specified the price but did not mention the quality of the logs. The parties had a dispute over quality and P sued for the purchase price. The trial court, over P's objection, allowed D to offer oral testimony that there was a warranty. When D prevailed, P sought a new trial. The court refused. P appeals.

Issue. May parol evidence be admitted to prove the existence of a warranty when the sales contract was silent about any warranty?

Held. No. Judgment reversed.

♦   The basic rule is that parol contemporaneous evidence is inadmissible to contradict or vary the terms of a valid written instrument. Parol evidence also cannot be admitted to show that the parties did not intend the written contract to be complete.

♦   The agreement in this case appears on its face to be a complete expression of the whole agreement of the parties. Parol evidence might be used to provide a better understanding of the language of the agreement, but cannot be used to provide new or different terms.

♦   Some cases hold that parol evidence of a warranty is admissible because a warranty is collateral to the terms of sale. It is collateral in the sense that title would pass without a warranty, but, when made, a warranty is part of a contract of sale. To the extent parol evidence can be used for collateral matters, the promise must relate to a subject distinct from that to which the writing relates.

c. **Any relevant evidence admitted.** Many courts now hold that *any* evidence may be admitted to determine whether the parties intended the contract as a final and complete expression of the agreement.

3. **Exceptions.** Parol evidence is admissible despite the existence of an integrated written contract in the following situations:

a. To show *sham, forgery, failure of consideration, or failure of conditions.*

b. To show *fraud, duress, or mistake.*

c. To prove the existence of a *condition precedent* to the legal effectiveness of a written contract.

d. To show that there was a *separate collateral parol agreement.* This requires evidence that: (i) the terms do not conflict with the written agreement; and (ii) the collateral agreement concerns a subject that the parties would not ordinarily be expected to include in the written agreement. Evidence of separate consideration is also important.

4. **Contract Interpretation.** Parol evidence may also be used to show what the parties meant by the words used in the writing.

a. **Custom or usage.** Parol evidence is admissible to show any *special meanings* attached to words used in the written agreement deriving from custom or usage in a particular industry. Under the U.C.C., this is expanded to include special meanings attached by virtue of previous dealings between the parties under other contracts, and by the parties' course of performance under the present contract. [*See* U.C.C. §2-202]

b. **Ambiguities.** If the agreement is ambiguous *on its face* or becomes ambiguous *in performance* (*e.g.,* D sells "my car," and it turns out she has two cars), parol evidence is admissible to clarify the parties' intent. Of course, if the ambiguity is so fundamental that there is no way that the court could determine what the parties intended, there may be no enforceable contract at all (*i.e.,* the terms may not be sufficiently definite to form a contract).

c. **Meaning of words.**

1) **Traditional rule.** Where there is no ambiguity or special meaning attached by custom or usage, the traditional rule has been that the terms of an agreement were to be interpreted according to their "plain meaning," on the rationale that the parties expected that they would be so interpreted.

2) **Modern rule.** There is an increasing tendency to be more liberal and allow parol evidence to show what the parties intended by their words, without regard to their "plain" meaning. Rationale: No language is infallible; what is "plain" to the judge may not have been "plain" to the parties. This approach has been criticized, because the process of interpretation can be misused to vary or contradict the terms of the written instrument. Either party can always claim that she "did not mean" what she said, and to allow parol evidence in such cases can effectively destroy the rule.

d.   Ambiguity based on the context--

Taylor v. State Farm Mutual Automobile Insurance Co., 854 P.2d 1134 (Ariz. 1993).

Facts. Taylor (P) was involved in a three-car collision. P was sued by one of the other drivers, who had previously settled with the third driver. P was defended by his own attorney as well as a lawyer for P's insurer, State Farm Mutual Automobile Insurance Co. (D). The jury awarded damages that exceeded P's insurance policy limits by $2.5 million. P sued D for bad faith, claiming D had improperly failed to settle the case within policy limits. D sought summary judgment based on a release P had signed to get D to pay $15,000 in uninsured motorist benefits. The trial court found that the release was ambiguous and allowed parol evidence to help interpret the release. The jury awarded P $2.1 million, plus $300,000 in attorney fees. The court of appeals reversed on the ground that the release agreement was not ambiguous. The Arizona Supreme Court granted review.

Issue. May extrinsic evidence be used to interpret the meaning of a release of "all contractual claims" when the plaintiff is suing an insurer on a bad faith theory?

Held. Yes. Judgment reversed.

♦   Interpretation may be a proper ground for using parol evidence. Under the restrictive "plain meaning" approach, parol evidence can be used for interpretation only where contract language is unclear, ambiguous, or vague. Under the rule of the Second Restatement and Professor Corbin, a judge can consider extrinsic evidence to determine whether it is relevant to the parties' intent, then applies the parol evidence rule to exclude from the fact finder's consideration only evidence that contradicts or varies the meaning of the agreement.

♦   In Arizona, a court may consider surrounding circumstances, including negotiations, prior understandings, and subsequent conduct to interpret a contract. Following Corbin's approach, a court must consider the evidence and then eliminate evidence that is not probative in determining the parties' intent. Then the court interprets the contract with this evidence, without admitting extrinsic evidence that would vary or contradict the meaning of the written words.

♦   The objective is to ascertain and give effect to the parties' intentions, including any special meanings of words. To do this, the courts should consider offered evidence and, if the contract language is "reasonably susceptible" to the proposed interpretation, the evidence can be admitted to help with interpretation.

♦   In this case, P released "all contractual rights, claims and causes of action" against D in connection with the collision and all subsequent matters. P argues that the bad faith claim is a tort claim, not a contract claim. The court of appeals held that P's claim was only contractual, but the legal character of bad faith is not universally established, so P's interpretation is reasonable and the trial court was correct that the language is ambiguous.

♦   There is sufficient extrinsic evidence to support P's interpretation, including the parties' knowledge of the size of the judgment against P and the use of limiting language in the release. The release did not refer to tort claims or bad faith. The trial court properly submitted the interpretation issue to the jury, and the evidence supports the verdict.

---

5.   Fraud Allegation Superseded by Writing--

Sherrodd, Inc. v. Morrison-Knudsen Co., 815 P.2d 1135 (Mont. 1991).

Facts. Sherrodd, Inc. (P) subcontracted with COP Construction to do earthmoving work for the construction of family housing. COP was a subcontractor to Morrison-Knudsen Co. (D), the general contractor. D's agent told P's officer that there were 25,000 cubic yards of excavation to be performed. P made its bid based on D's statement. While performing the work, P discovered that there was much more than 25,000 cubic yards of work to do. The contract provided that P had examined the site and had no verbal agreement with anyone that would affect or modify any of the terms of the written contract. It also provided that the contract was comprehensive and conclusive, and that no changes would be permitted unless signed by both parties. After doing the work, P sued to set aside the price provisions of the contract and to recover quantum meruit plus tort damages. The court granted D summary judgment based on the parol evidence rule. P appeals.

Issue. May the fraud exception to the parol evidence rule be asserted when a construction contract states that the plaintiff examined the site and satisfied himself as to the character, quantity, and kinds of materials to be encountered?

Held. No. Judgment affirmed.

♦   P's claim that D misled P about the amount of work to be done is contradicted by P's representation in the contract that P had examined the property and satisfied itself as to the amount of work to be done. P's claim is also superseded by the contract's clause stating that all negotiations and agreements prior to the date of the contract were merged in the writing.

♦   P claims that COP officers induced P to sign the contract by promising to pay more than the contract price, but this claim is also superseded by the written contract that specifies no changes would be valid unless reduced to writing.

Dissent. The majority opinion means that no party can be held liable for fraud so long as it is in a sufficiently advantageous bargaining position as to compel the other party to sign a contract that extinguishes liability for fraud. The majority ignores the fraud exception in U.C.C. section 2-905(2).

---

6. **Implied Duty to Act in Accordance with Trade Usage--**

Nanakuli Paving & Rock Co. v. Shell Oil Co., 664 F.2d 772 (9th Cir. 1981).

Facts. Nanakuli Paving & Rock Co. (P) was an asphalt paver that bought all of its asphalt requirements from Shell Oil Co. (D). The supply contracts between P and D specified that the price would be D's posted price at the time of delivery. However, all material suppliers to the asphalt paving industry followed a trade practice of price protection, whereby suppliers would charge pavers the price in effect when the pavers bid on the particular project involved. Most contracts were with government agencies that did not permit escalation clauses. On two prior occasions, D in fact provided price protection for P by extending the old price for four months and three months, respectively. However, D suddenly raised the price of asphalt from $44 to $76 after P already had a contract for which it needed 7,200 tons of asphalt. P sued, claiming D breached its contract. The jury found for P, but the trial court granted judgment n.o.v. P appeals.

Issue. May a contract term that specifically provides for a price to be established as of the date of delivery be modified by the trade usage and course of performance of the parties?

Held. Yes. Judgment reversed and jury verdict reinstated.

♦ The evidence presented at trial showed that asphalt suppliers routinely protected pavers from price changes. The suppliers would give advance notice of price increases, and would charge the old price for work committed at that price. The system worked because the market was so small.

♦ D claims that the trade usage should extend only to sellers of asphalt, of which there were only two: D and Chevron. However, usage of trade is not limited to members of the party's own trade, if it is so commonly practiced in a locality that a party should be aware of it. D constantly dealt with P in a small market and should have been aware of P's practice of making fixed price bids based on price protection from suppliers. The definition of trade to include all suppliers was not incorrect. In addition, the practice was virtually universal and D could not show one instance of a supplier failing to price protect a paver before its own failure to do so.

- D also claims that its two instances of giving P price protection does not constitute a course of performance. While it is a general rule that one instance does not constitute a course of performance, two may, especially when they were the only two occasions that necessitated such conduct. Nor were these two instances waivers as a matter of law. The jury could determine whether they were simply waivers of the contract terms or actually a course of performance of the contract. The jury's findings are supported by the evidence.

- D argues that the express terms are inconsistent with the usage in course of performance. Under the U.C.C., the parties' agreement may be more than the written words; it may include other circumstances such as course of performance and usage of trade. The latter are not binding only if they cannot be reasonably reconciled with the express contract terms. The price protection usage was not a total negation of the price-setting term, as would be, for example, a usage that the buyer set the price. While the usage is a broad exception to that term, it does not eliminate it entirely. For that reason, the jury could have found that price protection was reasonably consistent with the express price term.

- D had a duty to act in good faith, specifically, a duty to fix a price in good faith, under U.C.C. section 2-305(2). While a posted price normally satisfies this requirement, D's manner of carrying out the price increase did not comply with commercially reasonable standards. D did not give appropriate advance notice and did not price-protect P.

Concurrence. The practice of price protection was a well-established one about which the parties knew, or should have known. This case does not stand for a general rule that good faith requires price protection.

VI. SUPPLEMENTING THE AGREEMENT: IMPLIED TERMS, THE OBLIGATION OF GOOD FAITH, AND WARRANTIES

A. THE RATIONALE FOR IMPLIED TERMS

1. **Introduction.** Even where a bilateral contract apparently contains no promise at all on one side (*i.e.*, there is a complete lack of mutuality), the contract may still be upheld if the surrounding facts and the nature of the agreement fairly imply a promise of performance by that party.

2. **Implication of Reasonable Efforts--**

Wood v. Lucy, Lady Duff-Gordon, 118 N.E. 214 (N.Y. 1917).

Facts. Wood (P) was given an exclusive contract to place the endorsement of Lucy, Lady Duff-Gordon (D) on the designs of other clothiers and to place D's own designs on sale and to license others to sell them. D was to receive one-half of P's profits. The contract indicated that P had an organization capable of performing the contract, but it did not expressly indicate that P would perform. P sued D for breach of the contract on the basis that D put her endorsement on clothes of a competitor without P's knowledge and without sharing the profits with P. D demurred, claiming that the agreement lacked the elements of a contract since P bound himself to nothing. P appeals a dismissal of the complaint.

Issue. Where P did not specifically promise to use reasonable efforts to promote D's goods, and all compensation to D under the contract was to come from such efforts, was there a valid promise by P?

Held. Yes. Judgment reversed.

♦   A promise that P will use reasonable efforts to promote D's goods may be fairly implied. The circumstances of the contract make such an implication reasonable.

♦   It was an exclusive dealing contract that D gave to P, and any return to D was to come from P's profits. This means that if D was to get anything at all, P had to perform.

3. Implication of Reasonable Notification--

Leibel v. Raynor Manufacturing Co., 571 S.W.2d 640 (Ky. Ct. App. 1978).

Facts. Leibel (P) and Raynor Manufacturing Co. (D) entered an oral agreement to give P an exclusive dealer-distributorship for D's garage doors. P borrowed substantial amounts of money to make capital expenditures, purchase inventory, and have working capital. After two years of declining sales, D notified P that it was terminating the relationship and giving the distributorship to a third party. P sued for breach of contract. D moved for summary judgment, asserting that the agreement was for an indefinite duration and could be terminated at will by either party. The trial court granted summary judgment for D, holding that the U.C.C. did not apply, but that even if it did, it only required actual notice, which D did provide. P appeals.

Issue. Must reasonable notification be given to terminate an ongoing oral agreement for the sale of goods in a relationship between the manufacturer and a dealer-distributor?

Held. Yes. Judgment reversed.

♦   Article II of the U.C.C. applies to transactions involving goods and merchandise. A distributorship agreement involves the sale of goods and is therefore covered by the U.C.C.

♦   Under U.C.C. section 2-309(2), a contract with indefinite duration is valid for a reasonable time but can be terminated at any time by either party, but only by giving reasonable notification. Principles of good faith and sound commercial practice require such notification as will give the terminated party reasonable time to seek a substitute arrangement.

♦   What length of time constitutes reasonable notice depends on the facts of each situation, so it was not appropriate to grant summary judgment.

Comment. In some states, the law provides a requirement that a dealership contract cannot be terminated without sufficient notice to allow the dealer to recoup its investment.

B. THE IMPLIED OBLIGATION OF GOOD FAITH

1. **Introduction.** Modern contract law imposes an obligation to perform in good faith. U.C.C. section 1-203 provides that every contract or duty within the U.C.C. imposes an obligation of good faith in its performance or enforce-

ment. The Restatement (Second) of Contracts section 205, likewise says that "[e]very contract imposes upon each party a duty of good faith and fair dealing in its performance and its enforcement." A party can breach the duty of good faith even without breaching any explicit contractual provision.

2. Obligation of Good Faith Implied in Every Contract--

Seidenberg v. Summit Bank, 791 A.2d 1068 (N.J. Super. Ct. App. Div. 2002).

Facts. Seidenberg and his partner (Ps) sold their stock in health insurance brokerage corporations they had formed to Summit Bank (D) in exchange for stock in D's parent corporation. D agreed to retain Ps in their executive positions and to work with Ps to expand the brokerage business. Ps sued, alleging that D failed to perform in these areas, depriving Ps of certain income and involvement in the business. The parties settled all claims except P's claim that D breached the implied covenant of good faith and fair dealing. D moved for dismissal. The judge granted the motion on the ground that Ps were actually seeking to enforce an oral agreement outside the written agreement, in violation of the parol evidence rule. Ps appeal.

Issues.

(i) Does an implied covenant of good faith and fair dealing arise even when the parties have equal bargaining power?

(ii) Does the implied covenant of good faith and fair dealing permit the inclusion of terms and conditions that were not expressly set forth in the written contract?

Held. (i) Yes. (ii) Yes. Judgment reversed and case remanded.

♦ In New Jersey, all contracts contain a covenant of good faith and fair dealing. Neither party can do anything that has the effect of destroying or injuring the other party's right to receive the fruits of the contract.

♦ The implied covenant of good faith and fair dealing allows courts to adjust contractual obligations. Some courts have focused on inadequate bargaining power or financial vulnerability, such as in *Sons of Thunder v. Borden, Inc.*, 690 A.2d 575 (N.J. 1997). Others have focused on the parties' expectations or the defendant's bad faith or outright dishonesty. However, the covenant's existence does not arise solely from the plaintiffs' financial vulnerability, and the parol evidence rule does not preclude application of the covenant in a case such as this.

♦ In this case, Ps are experienced in the industry and had sufficient bargaining power when the contract was formed. Although economic dependency was a key factor in *Sons of Thunder*, disparate strength is not an essential element of a cause of action based on good faith performance.

♦ The parol evidence rule cannot inhibit the application of the implied covenant of good faith and fair dealing because that covenant is contained in all New Jersey contracts by operation of law. The implied covenant of good faith and fair dealing permits the inclusion of terms and conditions that were not in the written contract. It allows redress for bad faith performance that is not a breach of any express term. The covenant also permits courts to inquire into a party's exercise of discretion granted by the contract. The implied covenant cannot alter or override an express term, but it requires parties to act in good faith.

♦ The parol evidence rule prevents the court from altering a written contract, but that relates to the creation of the contract. The rule cannot eliminate the implied covenant that is part of every contract. To determine whether the implied covenant has been breached, the courts must consider parol evidence.

♦ The covenant of good faith and fair dealing reflects the fundamental notion that a party may not unreasonably frustrate the purpose of the contract. It applies when the contract does not include a term necessary to fulfill the parties' expectations, when one party resorts to bad faith in exercising a contractual right to terminate, and when the contract expressly provides a party with discretion as to its performance.

♦ In this case, Ps have alleged facts that fit the last two situations. Ps claim that their employment agreements contained a minimum term of five years and provided that, in the absence of termination by D, their employment would continue until each reached the age of 70. Ps also claim that D failed to pursue or create leads, frustrated or delayed marketing efforts, and deprived Ps of information that might have improved their benefits under the contract. They have also alleged the necessary element of bad faith, which in this context requires a violation of any commercially reasonable standard. Because Ps have alleged a cause of action, the motion to dismiss should not have been granted.

_____

3. **Conditions of Satisfaction and Good Faith.**

    a. **Introduction.** A condition may require performance to the "satisfaction" of another party. For example, if A promises to paint B's house and B promises to pay A $1,000 if "I am satisfied with the work," B's being satisfied is a condition precedent to having to pay the $1,000. The issue is always one of how "satisfaction" is to be measured.

    b. **Where the parties specify subjective "satisfaction."** In some contracts, the contract specifically mentions that satisfaction is "my personal satisfaction" (*i.e.,* subjective satisfaction of one of the parties). Normally, courts read the word "satisfied" literally and the party is under no obligation to pay unless he is personally satisfied.

c. **Where the standard of satisfaction is not specified.** Other contracts use the word satisfaction without specifically indicating that it is the personal satisfaction of one of the parties; *i.e.,* if the work is performed "satisfactorily," etc. In this case, the basis for determining satisfactory performance depends on the context of the contract.

1) **Where the subject matter of the contract is not personal.** In contracts where the subject matter is not "personal," such as with construction contracts, satisfaction tends to be read as a performance that would satisfy a "reasonable person."

2) **Where the subject matter is personal.** In these situations, such as with a contract to paint a portrait, the courts hold that personal satisfaction is required.

d. **Application in commercial construction--**

Morin Building Products Co. v. Baystone Construction, Inc., 717 F.2d 413 (7th Cir. 1983).

Facts. Baystone Construction, Inc. (D) was hired by General Motors to build an addition to a Chevrolet plant. The walls were to be built of aluminum with a mill finish. D hired Morin Building Products Co. (P) to supply and erect the walls. P's contract provided that all work would be done subject to the final approval of General Motors's agent, whose decision in matters relating to artistic effect would be final. The decision of acceptability would rest strictly with General Motors. P erected the walls, but in bright sunlight they did not have a uniform appearance. General Motors rejected the work and D hired a replacement subcontractor. P sued for the balance of the contract price ($23,000). The judge instructed the jury that the satisfaction clause must be interpreted by an objective standard; *i.e.,* whether a reasonable owner should have been satisfied with the work. The jury found for P. D appeals.

Issue. Does a subjective standard apply to a satisfaction clause in a commercial building contract for a factory wall that does not require a painted finish or other aesthetic qualities?

Held. No. Judgment affirmed.

♦ If the jury instruction was correct, the verdict was supported by the evidence, but if the jury should have applied a subjective standard based solely on good faith, a new trial would be required.

♦ The majority approach is to follow the objective rule in the absence of explicit language otherwise, so long as objective standards are available to guide the factfinder. This gives effect to the reasonable expectations of the parties. Objective standards may include commercial quality, operative fitness, or mechanical utility.

♦ For the subject of the contract—a factory wall—aesthetic considerations were far less important than function and cost. This is not a contract for a portrait painting, where the good faith subjective standard would apply.

♦ The contract provided for unpainted mill-finish aluminum, which is not usually uniform. If General Motors wanted a uniform finish, they would probably have specified a painted finish.

♦ The reasonableness of P's work can be evaluated by objective standards of satisfactory commercial quality. However, the contract in this case includes terms that suggest a subjective good faith standard. But these appear to be part of the form contract and it is not clear that they were intended to apply to the aesthetics of a mill-finish aluminum factory wall.

♦ It is unlikely that P intended to bind itself to a standard higher than matching the finish of existing metal siding, as expressly required by the contract. It is not known how important to General Motors the aesthetics were, but if it really was important, the contract would not have been drafted as ambiguously as it was.

Comment. In *Forman v. Benson*, 446 N.E.2d 535 (Ill. Ct. App. 1983), the court noted that a defendant seller who asserted a right to subjective rejection of the plaintiff's creditworthiness acted in bad faith as evidenced by its attempt, prior to rejection, to renegotiate the purchase price.

---

4. Duty to Act in Good Faith in Exercising Discretion--

Locke v. Warner Bros., Inc., 66 Cal. Rptr. 2d 921 (Cal. Ct. App. 1997).

Facts. Locke (P) began a personal and romantic relationship with Clint Eastwood when they filmed the movie The Outlaw Josey Wales for Warner Bros., Inc. (D). P and Eastwood lived together for about 12 years before Eastwood terminated their relationship. The parties reached a property settlement that included a development deal for P with D. The contract required D to pay P $250,000 per year for three years for "first look" rights, whereby P had to give D a chance to approve or reject any movie that P was interested in developing. P also received a $750,000 "pay or play" directing deal that required D to pay P whether she directed a movie or not. Secretly, Eastwood promised to reimburse D for the cost of the contract if P did not succeed in getting projects produced and developed. D paid P the full $1.5 million required but did not develop any of her projects or hire her to direct any movies. P sued, claiming the development deal was a sham because D did not intend to make movies with her but only wanted to help Eastwood settle with P. P offered deposition testimony that one of D's executives said D was not going to work with P, and that P's development deal was "Clint's deal." The trial court granted D's motion for summary judgment, holding that an implied covenant of good faith could not be imposed where the contract did not require D to have a good faith basis for declining to accept P's development projects. P appeals.

Issue. Where a contract confers on one party a discretionary power affecting the rights of the other, is there an implied duty to act in good faith in exercising that discretion?

Held. Yes. Judgment reversed.

◆ Every contract contains an implied covenant that neither party shall do anything that will have the effect of impairing the other party's right to receive the benefits of the contract.

◆ This contract gave D the right to make a subjective creative decision. Such a decision cannot be reviewed by the courts for reasonableness. However, the implied duty of good faith requires that D's dissatisfaction be actual or genuine. D was not required to accept P's projects if D was not satisfied with them, so long as D acted in good faith. D could not reject P's projects in bad faith.

◆ P offered testimony that D's executives knew D would never work with P. This raises a triable issue as to whether D categorically refused to work with P, regardless of the merits of her proposals, which would be a violation of the contract.

◆ Implied terms cannot be used by the courts to change express terms. In this case, however, the contract did not give D the express right to refrain from working with P. It merely gave D discretion with respect to developing P's projects, so that an implied covenant of good faith and fair dealing can be imposed to require D to exercise its discretion in good faith.

◆ P's evidence also creates a factual question about whether D entered the contract with fraudulent intent.

---

5. **Limit on Implied Good Faith Requirement in At-Will Employment Relationship--**

Donahue v. Federal Express Corp., 753 A.2d 238 (Pa. Super. Ct. 2000).

Facts. Donahue (P) worked for Federal Express Corp. (D) for over 11 years as an at-will employee. P noticed errors on repair invoices and complained that his supervisor was sending auto body work to the supervisor's friend's auto body shop. P was fired within a few months. After exhausting his administrative remedies within D's policies and procedures, P sued for wrongful termination. D demurred. The trial court granted judgment to D. P appeals.

Issue. Is there an implied covenant of good faith that applies to at-will employment relationships?

Held. No. Judgment affirmed.

♦ The law imposes a duty of good faith on both parties to a contract in the performance and enforcement of the contract. If an at-will employment relationship includes contract terms beyond the at-will employment, the duty of good faith applies to those terms. However, the courts do not recognize an implied duty of good faith to a termination of a pure at-will employment relationship.

♦ P claims that D violated the duty of good faith in its treatment of his appeal under D's policies and procedures. Those policies expressly state that they do not create contractual rights regarding termination, so there are no contractual terms to which the duty of good faith can apply.

♦ P asserts that he was terminated as a whistle-blower, in violation of public policy. However, there are no statutes or legal precedents that prohibit private companies from firing employees for reporting unscrupulous practices.

♦ Finally, P claims that he provided sufficient additional consideration to overcome the presumption that he is an at-will employee, the consideration being superior job performance. Such an allegation is insufficient to establish additional consideration.

C. WARRANTIES

1. **Introduction.** Every contract for the sale of goods includes a warranty that the seller has good title to the goods. [U.C.C. §2-312]

    a. **Warranty of merchantability.** A merchant seller also warrants, by implication, that goods sold are "merchantable," meaning that they meet basic standards including fitness for their ordinary purposes. [U.C.C. §2-314]

    b. **Warranty of fitness for a particular purpose.** If a seller has reason to know that the buyer intends to use the goods for a particular purpose and that the buyer is relying on the seller to select suitable goods, the seller warrants by implication that the goods are fit for a particular purpose. [U.C.C. §2-315]

    c.   **Disclaimers and limitation of remedies.** A seller may disclaim implied warranties with specific and conspicuous language. [*See* U.C.C. §2-316]. Under U.C.C. section 2-719(1)(a), a seller can also limit the buyer's remedies for breach of warranty, so long as the exclusive remedy does not fail of its essential purpose or there is no personal injury.

2.   General Product Information--

Bayliner Marine Corp. v. Crow, 509 S.E.2d 499 (Va. 1999).

Facts. Crow (P) was invited to ride on a new sport fishing boat manufactured by Bayliner Marine Corp. (D). D's dealer gave P printed information from D's dealer's manual that gave the specifications for its boats, including a maximum speed of 30 miles per hour for a boat with a specified prop. P purchased a boat that came with 2,000 pounds of optional equipment and a different prop. When he piloted it for the first time, the maximum speed P could reach was 13 miles per hour. D's dealer worked on it and was able to deliver a maximum speed of 24 miles per hour. D told P that the performance representations he had originally seen were incorrect and that 23 to 25 miles per hour was the maximum possible speed. P sued for breach of express warranties and implied warranties of merchantability and fitness for a particular purpose. The trial court awarded P the purchase price of $120,000 plus $15,000 in incidental expenses. D appeals.

Issue. Does a manufacturer make an express warranty to a purchaser about a specific boat when it provides information about the performance of its products that are configured differently from the purchaser's boat?

Held. No. Judgment reversed.

♦   D's dealer's manual specified performance for boats based on their prop size. P purchased a boat that had a smaller prop than that described in D's manual. The boat described in D's manual also did not have all the extra equipment that P purchased. Therefore, D's manual did not constitute an express warranty as to P's boat.

♦   D's sales brochure stated that the boat would deliver "the kind of performance you need to get to the prime offshore fishing grounds." P claims that this constitutes an express warranty. However, under U.C.C. section 2-313(2), a statement purporting to be merely the seller's opinion or commendation of the goods does not create a warranty. The statement in the brochure does not describe a specific characteristic of the boat, but is merely D's opinion about the quality of the boat's performance. The brochure did not create an express warranty.

♦   P claims that D breached an implied warranty of merchantability because the boat's slow speed made it difficult to get from one fishing spot to another quickly. Under U.C.C. section 2-314, goods are merchantable if they "are fit for the ordinary purposes for which such goods are used." P is required to establish the standard of merchantability in the trade, but he failed to do this, or to show that a significant portion of the boat-buying public would object to purchasing an offshore fishing boat with the speed capability P's boat had. The boat's being slower than P wanted does not make the boat not merchantable.

♦   P used the boat for 850 hours of engine time, which shows that the boat was fit for its purpose as a fishing boat. P did not prove that he made known to D that P intended to use the boat to go 30 miles per hour. D could not know that, on the date of sale, a boat incapable of traveling at 30 miles per hour was unacceptable to P.

---

3.   Housing Merchant Warranty--

Caceci v. Di Canio Construction Corp., 526 N.E.2d 266 (N.Y. 1988).

Facts. In 1976, the Cacecis (Ps) contracted with Di Canio Construction Corp. (D) to purchase land and have D build a single-family home. The total price was $55,000, and D gave a one-year guarantee on the house, limiting D's liability to replacement or repair of any defects or defective parts. Four years after the title closed, Ps noticed a dip in the kitchen floor that D attempted to fix. Although D claimed the dip was due to ordinary settling, Ps discovered that the problem was that the topsoil under the house contained tree trunks and other biodegradable materials that were deteriorating. They had to tear up the foundation and replace it. In 1983, Ps sued, claiming breach of contract, negligent construction, and breach of implied warranty of workmanlike construction. The court rejected all claims except the breach of implied warranty. The court awarded Ps the cost of repair, which was over $57,000. The appellate division affirmed. D appeals.

Issue. To prove a breach of an implied housing merchant warranty, must the plaintiff show that the builder had knowledge of the defect?

Held. No. Judgment affirmed.

♦   The lower courts based the judgment on the implied warranty theory on the ground that D knew the house was being built on poor soil. Under an implied housing merchant warranty, however, there is no requirement that the builder-vendor have knowledge of a latent defect.

◆ This implied warranty is an extension of the implied warranty that attends the sale of chattels. The doctrine of caveat emptor no longer applies to the sale of new homes by the builder.

◆ The rationale for this implied warranty is the buyer's inability to discover defects and the builder-vendor's superior position in preventing the occurrence of major defects. Sound contract principles, policy, and fairness require that the responsibility and liability in this type of case be placed on the party best able to prevent and bear the loss.

◆ D claims that only the legislature should decide how to allocate the respective duties in this type of case, but the doctrine of implied warranty was originally created by the courts and the common law continues to adapt to new situations.

Comment. Only a few states have so far declined to adopt an implied warranty of workmanship in the sale of a new home by the builder. The warranty normally includes two elements: the house must be habitable and it must be free from defects in construction.

VII. AVOIDING ENFORCEMENT: INCAPACITY, BARGAINING MIS- CONDUCT, UNCONSCIONABILITY, AND PUBLIC POLICY

A. MINORITY AND MENTAL INCAPACITY

1. **Introduction.** The basic rule for a contract entered into by a minor is that if the contract is for a necessary good or service, it is enforceable; if it is prejudicial to the minor, it is void; and if it is unclear whether it is beneficial or prejudicial, the contract is voidable at the election of the minor.

2. **The Benefit Rule for Purchases by Minors--**

Dodson v. Shrader, 824 S.W.2d 545 (Tenn. 1992).

Facts. Dodson (P) purchased a used pickup truck from the Shraders (Ds). P was 16 years old at the time. He paid $4,900 in cash. Ds believed P was 18 or 19, but did not specifically inquire about P's age. Nine months later, the truck had serious engine problems that P could not afford to fix. P drove the truck another month until the engine stopped working. P asked Ds for a refund. Ds refused to take the truck back or give a refund. P sued to rescind the contract and recover the purchase price. At trial, Ds showed that the truck was worth only $500 in its present condition. The court found for P and ordered Ds to return the purchase price to P. The court of appeals affirmed. Ds appeal.

Issue. May a minor void a contract and insist on a return of the full purchase price even if he damages the goods while they were in his possession?

Held. No. Judgment reversed and case remanded.

♦ The traditional rule regarding minors and contracts has been modified to allow the minor to determine whether a contract is favorable or not by making the contract voidable by the minor.

♦ Although the minor has the right to void a contract, a minor may not use this right as a means for injuring others who dealt with him in good faith. Some states have adopted limits on the right of rescission. Under the benefit rule, upon rescission of a contract by a minor, recovery of the full purchase price is subject to a deduction for the minor's use of the goods. The minor's recovery is also subject to a deduction for depreciation or deterioration of the goods while in the minor's possession.

- In modern times, people between 18 and 21 years of age are assuming more responsibilities in their lives than the same aged people in previous years. Accordingly, the following rule shall apply in Tennessee. Where a minor party to a contract has not been overreached in any way, there has been no undue influence, the contract is fair and reasonable, and the minor paid money on the purchase price and used the goods purchased, the minor may not rescind and recover the amount actually paid without a deduction for the use of the goods, depreciation, and willful or negligent damage to the goods.

- In this case, P used the truck and damaged it by continuing to operate it after being told that he should not. He left it in an area where the truck was damaged by a hit-and-run driver. The trier of fact should consider the amount of the damage to the truck and the relative liability for that damage between the parties.

---

3. Borrower's Mental Capacity--

Hauer v. Union State Bank of Wautoma, 532 N.W.2d 456 (Wis. Ct. App. 1995).

Facts. Hauer (P) suffered brain damage in a motorcycle accident and was adjudicated to be incompetent. The court-appointed guardianship was subsequently terminated based on P's doctor's opinion that P had recovered sufficiently to manager her own affairs. P's monthly income was $900 per month. Eilbes defaulted on a loan he had received from Union State Bank of Wautoma (D). Eilbes met P and suggested that P take out a loan using her mutual fund account as collateral. Eilbes arranged for D to extend a $30,000 loan to P, despite P having told D that P lived on the income generated from the mutual fund. When the loan became due and Eilbes was filing bankruptcy, P sued D on the ground that D knew or should have known that P lacked the mental capacity to understand the loan. At trial, the jury found for P. The trial court entered judgment for P, voiding the loan contract and ordering D to return P's collateral. D appeals.

Issue. May a loan agreement be voided when the lender knew the borrower lacked sufficient mental capacity to enter the agreement, even where the borrower has spent the money?

Held. Yes. Judgment affirmed.

- Mental incompetence is not only an affirmative defense; it can be used by an incompetent to void a contract entirely. Therefore, P's complaint properly stated a cause of action.

- There is a presumption that every adult person is fully competent in the absence of satisfactory proof to the contrary. P thus had the burden to prove incompetence. The test is whether P had sufficient mental ability to know what she was doing and the nature and consequences of the transaction.

♦ In this case, P showed that she had been under a court-appointed guardianship about one year before D loaned her the money. P's testimony demonstrated a complete lack of understanding of the nature and consequences of the loan transaction. P's expert witness testified that P was very deficient in her cognitive ability and was gullible. This evidence suffices to uphold the jury verdict.

♦ The infancy doctrine allows an infant to disaffirm a contract even if the minor cannot return the property. The mental incapacity doctrine, however, allows a contract to be voided only if avoidance accords with equitable principles, unless there was fraud or knowledge of the incapacity by the other contracting party. This reflects the reality that there are varying degrees of infirmity, and seeks a fair balance between the competing interests when, as here, P cannot return any of the loan proceeds.

♦ The jury found that D failed to act in good faith when it loaned the money to P. Under the U.C.C., there is no requirement of good faith in the negotiation and formation of a contract; the good faith requirement is limited to performance or enforcement of a contract. However, good faith is relevant to P's attempt to void the contract. Under common law, there is a duty of good faith in every contract.

♦ Where a contract is made on fair terms and the other party has no reason to know of P's incompetency, the contract is not voidable if performance in whole or in part makes it impossible for the parties to be restored to their previous positions. In this case, there is sufficient evidence to support the jury's finding that D knew, was put on notice, or had reason to suspect P's incompetence.

Comment. In this case, D failed to request a special verdict question regarding whether D knew about P's incompetence. The special verdict form did not ask about D's knowledge. D does not have an affirmative duty to inquire into the mental capacity of an applicant for a loan, but if D was put on notice or given a reason to suspect P's incompetence, D should have inquired further.

B. DURESS AND UNDUE INFLUENCE

1. **Introduction.** A contract may be voidable if one party's consent was obtained by wrongful threats from the other party. Traditionally, this rule required a threat of personal injury. It has been expanded to include economic duress. However, a mere threat to refuse to enter a contract, or to agree only to disproportionately favorable terms, is not duress because there is no general duty to enter into a contract.

2. Economic Duress and Business Compulsion--

Totem Marine Tug & Barge, Inc. v. Alyeska Pipeline Service Co., 584 P.2d 15 (Alaska 1978).

Facts. Totem Marine Tug & Barge, Inc. (P) contracted to transport pipeline construction materials from Texas to Alaska for Alyeska Pipeline Service Co. (D). P charged a barge and an oceangoing tug to perform the contract. When P started performing, it discovered that D had around 7,000 tons of material to ship from Texas instead of the planned 2,000, which caused a month's delay for handling. The extra load slowed the vessels, so P chartered a second tug. D delayed signing an amendment to cover the cost of the tug, which delayed its passage through the Panama Canal. D then off-loaded P's vessels in Long Beach, California, and terminated the contract. P submitted invoices of nearly $300,000. P needed immediate payment to avoid bankruptcy, but D delayed payment. D offered a settlement of $97,500, which P accepted. P and its creditors later sued D, seeking rescission of the settlement on the ground of economic duress. D moved for summary judgment. The court granted D's motion. P appeals.

Issue. May a contract be rendered void under the economic duress doctrine if P could have sued D for the money D owed to P?

Held. Yes. Judgment reversed and case remanded.

♦   At early common law, the only duress that would justify avoiding a contract was a fear of loss of life or limb, mayhem, or imprisonment, where the threat was sufficient to overcome the will of a person of ordinary firmness and courage. The doctrine has been expanded to include economic coercion.

♦   There are several ways to describe economic duress. Duress exists where: (i) one party involuntarily accepted the terms of another; (ii) circumstances permitted no other alternative; and (iii) such circumstances were the result of coercive acts of the other party. Accordingly, P must show that D's wrongful acts or threats intentionally caused P to enter the transaction involuntarily. Some cases have held that a threat to breach a contract or to withhold payment of an admitted debt can suffice as a wrongful act.

♦   Economic duress does not arise merely because P was a victim of a wrongful act. P must have had no reasonable alternative but to agree to D's contract terms. Recourse to litigation might not be a reasonable alternative in some situations because of the inherent delays in collection through litigation.

♦   In this case, P's evidence, if believed by a jury, would support a finding that P executed the release under economic duress. D deliberately withheld payment of the debt, despite having acknowledged that debt. P was faced with impending bankruptcy that could be avoided only by accepting immediate cash payment from D.

---

3.   **Undue Influence--**

Odorizzi v. Bloomfield School District, 54 Cal. Rptr. 533 (Cal. Ct. App. 1966).

Facts. Odorizzi (P) was arrested for homosexual activities on June 10. On June 11, he resigned from his position as an elementary school teacher in response to statements from the school officials that if he did not resign, he would be dismissed and the charges against him would be publicized. In July, the criminal charges were dismissed. P sued the Bloomfield School District (D) to rescind his resignation because it was obtained by duress and undue influence. The trial court dismissed P's complaint. P appeals.

Issue. May a threat of termination for cause, made to obtain a resignation, constitute undue influence?

Held. Yes. Judgment reversed.

♦   There was no duress in this case because D had a legal right to threaten to dismiss P, and even had a positive duty to do so. So long as D acted in good faith, it could properly start dismissal proceedings, regardless of the impact on P's reputation.

♦   Unlike duress, undue influence is persuasion that is coercive in nature, characterized by high pressure that works on mental, moral, or emotional weakness. Misrepresentation of law or fact is not essential to a determination of undue influence. Most reported cases of undue influence involve confidential relationships, but this is not an essential element where the undue influence involves unfair advantage taken of another's weakness or distress.

♦   A critical element of undue influence is a lessened capacity of one party to make a free contract. It involves an unfair advantage attributable to a mismatch between the parties. It is not merely hindsight that makes one party wish to escape a bad bargain.

♦   The elements of undue influence include: (i) discussion of the transaction at an unusual or inappropriate time; (ii) consummation of the transaction in an unusual place; (iii) insistent demand that the deal be done at once; (iv) extreme emphasis on serious consequences of delay; (v) the use of multiple persuaders by the dominant side against a single servient party; (vi) absence of third-party advisors to the servient party; and (vii) statements that there is no time to consult advisors. The more of these factors that are present, the more likely the persuasion may be characterized as excessive.

♦ In this case, D sought to secure P's signature on the resignation, not his consent to his resignation. They assured P they were trying to help him, that he should rely on their advice, that there was not time to consult a lawyer, that dire consequences would immediately follow if he did not sign, and that if he resigned, the incident would not prevent him from getting a teaching job somewhere else. These elements were sufficient to raise a question about whether D had used undue influence to secure P's resignation.

C. MISREPRESENTATION AND NONDISCLOSURE

1. **Misrepresentation.** A contract is voidable by an innocent party who justifiably relies on a material misrepresentation made by another. The misrepresentation need not be fraudulent. It is enough if the misrepresentation would induce a reasonable person to agree, or the misrepresenting party knows that the misrepresentation would make the particular person agree. [*See* Restatement (Second) of Contracts §162]

2. **Sale of Unneeded Services--**

Syester v. Banta, 133 N.W.2d 666 (Iowa 1965).

Facts. Syester (P), a lonely and elderly widow, purchased dancing lessons from Banta (D), an owner of an Arthur Murray Dance Studio, over several years. P paid D a total of $29,174.30 for about 4,057 hours of lessons. This included three lifetime memberships. P used less than 10% of the hours she purchased. P sued for damages caused by D's fraudulent representations. At trial, P's former dancing instructor testified that P's level of dancing ability would require 200 to 400 hours of instruction and that she could not improve much because she was 68 years old. D had fired the instructor, but when P sued, D hired him back to persuade P to drop the lawsuit by flattering her and telling her she had the ability to be a professional dancer. D got P to settle for $6,090. P later signed a second release. D offered the releases as a complete defense. The jury found for P and awarded her $14,300 in actual damages and $40,000 in punitive damages. D appeals.

Issue. May a course of continually selling services to a customer who neither needs nor uses them, by falsely telling the customer that she can become a professional, constitute fraud?

Held. Yes. Judgment affirmed.

- D's course of conduct in this case was beyond the limits of propriety. Besides continually selling P dancing lessons that D knew she would not use, D falsely represented to P that she was improving and had the potential to become a professional dancer.

- D also induced P to enter the settlement agreements by manipulating her and leading her away from her own lawyer. This evidence supports the jury's verdict.

-----

3. **Nondisclosure.** The parties to a contract have no general obligation to disclose facts related to the subject matter of the contract, but there is a duty to disclose material facts if the parties have a relationship of trust or confidence. A party also has a duty to disclose material facts known due to her special position, where these facts could not be readily determined by the other party exercising normal diligence.

4. **Sale of Termite-Infested House--**

Hill v. Jones, 725 P.2d 1115 (Ariz. Ct. App. 1986).

Facts. The Hills (Ps) contracted to purchase a residence from the Joneses (Ds) for $72,000. Ds had to provide a termite inspection report that stated the property was free from evidence of termite infestation, which they did. During a visit prior to closing escrow, Ps noticed a ripple in the wood floor and asked if it could be termite damage. Mrs. Jones responded that it was water damage. Mr. Hill had seen similar ripples before that turned out to be termite damage, but he thought the termite report would reveal whether the ripple was due to termites or not. The termite report did not note physical damage or evidence of previous treatment. After Ps moved in, one of the neighbors told them the house had previously had a termite infestation. An exterminator confirmed the existence of termite damage and estimated the repair cost to be at least $5,000. Ps sued. During discovery, Ds disclosed that they and the prior owner had previously had the house treated for termites and had a guarantee from the exterminator. The termite inspector who had conducted the presale inspection claimed he should have been told about any history of termite infestation and treatment. The trial court granted summary judgment to Ds. Ps appeal.

Issue. Does the seller of a residence have a duty to disclose to the buyer facts pertaining to a past termite infestation?

Held. Yes. Judgment reversed and case remanded.

- The modern approach under Restatement (Second) section 161 places an affirmative duty on a vendor to disclose material facts if:

(i)   Disclosure is necessary to prevent a previous assertion from being a misrepresentation or from being fraudulent or material;

(ii)   Disclosure would correct a mistake of the other party as to a basic assumption on which that party is making the contract and if nondisclosure amounts to a failure to act in good faith and in accordance with reasonable standards of fair dealing;

(iii)   Disclosure would correct a mistake of the other party as to the contents or effect of a writing, evidencing or embodying an agreement in whole or in part; or

(iv)   The other person is entitled to know the fact because of a relationship of trust and confidence between them.

♦   Nondisclosure of a fact known to one party may sometimes be equivalent to the assertion that the fact does not exist, which may have the same legal effect as fraud and misrepresentation. In the context of residential home sales, a seller has a duty to disclose facts known to the seller that materially affect the value or desirability of the property and that are not known to or within the reach of the diligent observation of the buyer.

♦   The existence of termite infestation, whether ongoing or past, may be a material fact, depending on the circumstances. This is a question of fact that must be resolved by a jury. Questions about whether Ps had notice of possible termite infestation and their diligence in finding out more is also a jury question.

---

5.   Fraudulent Inducement--

Park 100 Investors, Inc. v. Kartes, 650 N.E.2d 347 (Ind. Ct. App. 1995).

Facts. Park 100 Investors, Inc. (P) prepared a lease agreement form for the Karteses (Ds), who wished to lease commercial space for their company. Ds signed the lease. The lease did not include any provisions for a personal guaranty of the lease. The day before Ds were to move into the space, P's agent told Ds that they had to sign additional lease papers or they could not move in. Given the urgency, Ds signed the document without reading it. In fact, the document was a personal guaranty of the lease. Years later, Ds discovered that they had signed a personal guaranty and they disavowed it. After Ds sold their interest in the company to a third party, the third party defaulted and P sued Ds on the guaranty. The trial court found that Ds were not liable. P appeals.

Issue. May a party enforce an agreement if it uses fraud to induce the other party to sign the agreement?

Held. No. Judgment affirmed.

- P's agent's statements that the personal guaranty was "lease papers" and that Ds could not move into the building until they signed the papers were each misrepresentations of material facts. P's agent made these false misrepresentations knowingly. Ds reasonably relied on P's agent's statements to their detriment.

- P claims that Ds had a duty to read the document and cannot avoid liability by claiming ignorance of its terms. While P's assertion is the normal rule, P itself used misrepresentations to induce Ds to obligate themselves. P cannot make a claim that Ds should have known better than to rely on P's representations.

- While a party has a duty to guard against fraud, the law does not ignore an intentional fraud practiced by the party seeking judicial enforcement of a contract. Under the facts in this case, P used fraud to obtain Ds' signatures on the personal guaranty, and therefore the courts will not hold Ds liable under that guaranty.

D. UNCONSCIONABILITY

1. **Introduction.** Under U.C.C. section 2-302, a contract that was unconscionable at the time it was made may be entirely unenforceable. A court can also partially enforce the contract by deleting unconscionable provisions, or it may limit the application of any unconscionable provisions.

   a. **Scope.** Although the U.C.C. applies only to the sale of goods, courts have applied the rule of unconscionability to all contracts.

   b. **Type of unconscionability.** Courts have recognized both procedural and substantive unconscionability. Procedural unconscionability arises when one party inserts a contract term that the other does not agree with and does not notice. This typically arises in adhesion contracts of insurance, consumer loans, and residential leases. Substantive unconscionability arises when a contract term itself is unconscionable.

2. **Unequal Bargaining Position--**

Williams v. Walker-Thomas Furniture Co., 350 F.2d 445 (D.C. Cir. 1965).

Facts. Walker-Thomas Furniture Co. (P) adopted a standard form contract for credit sales that provided that: (i) all credit transactions of a buyer were to be lumped into one account and each installment payment made was to be spread pro rata over all items being purchased (even when purchased at different times) until all items were paid off; and (ii) if purchaser defaulted, P could repossess all items. Williams (D) purchased several items on credit at different times. Eventually, she failed to make payments sufficient to cover the most recent item (a stereo). D was on welfare, separated from her husband, and caring for seven children. P brought an action to repossess all items D was purchasing on credit. The trial court granted judgment for P. The court of appeals affirmed. D appeals.

Issue. Is a seller's contract provision on repossession unconscionable where there is inequality of bargaining position?

Held. Yes. Judgment reversed and case remanded.

♦   Despite the common law rule of caveat emptor, some courts have held that unconscionable contracts are not enforceable as a matter of common law. This result has been codified in U.C.C. section 2-302. Accordingly, where a contract is unconscionable when it is made, it should not be enforced.

♦   The concept of unconscionability includes an absence of meaningful choice for one party combined with contract terms that are unreasonably favorable for the other party. The determination requires consideration of all the circumstances surrounding the transaction.

♦   D is in a poor economic class with little bargaining power. The gross inequality of bargaining position makes it possible for a sophisticated party such as P to exploit D by providing preprinted contracts containing unreasonable provisions. The lower courts did not make findings on the possible unconscionability of the contracts, so the case must be remanded.

Dissent. There was no sharp practice and D knew exactly where she stood. From a public policy standpoint, a cautious approach should be taken when resolving such problems, because the law has always given parties great latitude when making their own contracts.

Comment. Consider the policy considerations favoring P's position, given the risks of lending to welfare recipients. Some commentators argue that cases such as *Williams* and similar legislative efforts will restrict or even stop the flow of consumer goods to the poor.

---

3.   **Unilateral Arbitration Clause Unconscionable--**

Higgins v. Superior Court of Los Angeles County, 45 Cal. Rptr. 3d 293 (Cal. Ct. App. 2006).

Facts. The five Higgins siblings (Ps), whose parents had died, moved in with the Leomitis, a couple with three children of their own. The producers of the television program Extreme Makeover wanted to do a show about Ps, during which the Leomiti home would be completely renovated. Ps and the Leomitis signed an agreement regarding the show that included an arbitration provision. They also signed a release printed in a smaller font than the agreement. The release also provided for binding arbitration. No one discussed the arbitration clause with Charles, the oldest Higgins sibling, who was 21 and the guardian of his siblings. Ps allege that after the show was broadcast, the Leomiti couple told Ps that the house was theirs and forced Ps to move out. Ps sued the Leomitis and various entities involved with the production and broadcast of the program, who petitioned for arbitration. The trial court ordered arbitration. Ps petitioned for a writ of mandate challenging the trial court's arbitration order.

Issue. May an arbitration clause be deemed unconscionable where it requires only one party to submit its claims to arbitration?

Held. Yes. Writ of mandate granted.

◆ Although, generally, California favors arbitration, arbitration agreements are to be rescinded on the same grounds as other contract terms and are neither favored nor disfavored in this respect; they are treated like other contracts. They are valid unless there are grounds for revocation. One ground for revocation is unconscionability.

◆ The trial court found that Ps' challenge went to the agreement as a whole, which would be an issue for the arbitrator. However, Ps are challenging only the arbitration clause, not the entire agreement. The court also found that Ps had an opportunity to read the agreement and release. However, no authority has been cited stating that if a party reads an agreement, he is barred from claiming that it is unconscionable.

◆ Ps contend that the agreement and release are contracts of adhesion. A contract of adhesion is a standardized contract that is imposed and drafted by the party with superior bargaining strength and that gives the other party only the opportunity to adhere to the contract or reject it. If a court finds that a contract is adhesive, it must determine whether there are other factors that render it unenforceable.

◆ The agreement in this case is a standardized contract that was presented to Ps on a take-it-or-leave-it basis and was drafted by the television defendants, who had greater bargaining power than Ps and were unwilling to negotiate. The agreement is a contract of adhesion.

◆ Unconscionability has a procedural and a substantive element, both of which must be present to some degree for a court to refuse to enforce a contract or clause because of unconscionability.

- Procedural unconscionability focuses on factors of surprise and oppression. Here, the arbitration provision appears in an undistinguishable font as one of several paragraphs, with no highlighted text or place for initials next to the provision. The top of the first page of the agreement advises Ps to read the whole agreement, but this does not defeat the showing of procedural unconscionability.

- Substantive unconscionability reflects the one-sided nature of a contract provision. In this case, only Ps had to submit their claims to arbitration. The television defendants had the right to seek injunctive or other equitable relief in court, yet they could compel Ps to submit to arbitration. This constitutes substantive unconscionability.

---

4.   Arbitration Provisions Voided for Substantive Unconscionability--

Adler v. Fred Lind Manor, 103 P.3d 773 (Wash. 2004).

Facts. Fred Lind Manor (D) hired Adler (P) to work in maintenance at its senior citizen facility. A few years later, a management company hired by D required all employees to sign an arbitration agreement to remain employed. The agreement provided for a 180-day limitation on raising claims and required both parties to share the arbitrator's fee and other expenses of the arbitration process and to bear their own respective costs and attorneys' fees. P signed the agreement. Approximately six years later, P was injured when moving a commercial dryer at the general manager's direction. P filed claims for his injuries. D eventually terminated him in June 2002 for inability to perform all of the maintenance duties. In October 2002, P filed a complaint with the EEOC. D responded by asserting other reasons for the termination. Eventually the EEOC dismissed P's complaint. P filed a claim in state court in May 2003. D filed its answer in August 2003, claiming that P had to submit his claims to arbitration. D later informed P that it would seek dismissal of P's claim pursuant to the 180-day limitations clause. The trial court granted D's motion to compel arbitration. The Washington Supreme Court granted review.

Issue. May a contract provision be voided for substantive unconscionability alone?

Held. Yes. Case remanded.

- State law is preempted by federal law, and the Federal Arbitration Act requires arbitration when a valid arbitration agreement exists. Therefore, the Washington state law against discrimination cannot entitle P to a judicial forum.

- However, contract provisions may be rendered void if they are unconscionable. Although some jurisdictions require a showing of both procedural and substantive unconscionability, in Washington, substantive unconscionability alone may suffice to render a provision unconscionable.

- ◆ P asserts that the arbitration agreement was an adhesion contract and therefore unconscionable. We agree that the agreement was an adhesion contract, but a contract is not procedurally unconscionable just because it is an adhesion contract. Unequal bargaining power alone does not justify a finding of procedural unconscionability. The key is whether one party lacked meaningful choice. The facts surrounding the circumstances of the formation of the contract in this case are in dispute to a degree that more factual findings are required to determine whether procedural unconscionability exists in this case. Thus, we remand this case for additional findings.

- ◆ As for substantive unconscionability, the contract requires both parties to arbitrate claims. It is not a unilateral provision. The fee splitting provision could make the contract substantively unconscionable if, on remand, it turns out that arbitration involves prohibitive costs for P. However, the provision that prevents P from seeking to recover his attorney fees is a significant disadvantage compared with P's statutory right to attorney fees. This provision is substantively unconscionable.

- ◆ Although no statute prohibits parties from adopting a shorter limitation provision in their contracts, the 180-day limitation provision in this case is also substantively unconscionable. The provision requires a party to give written notice of his intention to seek arbitration no later than 180 days after the event that first gave rise to the dispute. This confers unfair advantages on D because it could force P to forgo other administrative actions and because it could bar claims arising out of discriminatory behavior that first began outside the limitations period.

- ◆ The unconscionable provisions can be severed from the overall agreement to arbitrate. On remand, the court should address P's claims of procedural unconscionability and of substantive unconscionability based on the fee-splitting provision.

Comment. *Adler* represents a departure from the majority rule that requires both substantive and procedural unconscionability to invalidate a contract.

E. PUBLIC POLICY

1. **Introduction.** At common law, courts occasionally refused to enforce contracts on grounds of public policy, such as contracts that called for excessive interest rates (usury) or restraint of trade. Many cases refer to this principle by calling the contract unenforceable because of "illegality," but the principle extends beyond matters that are strictly illegal.

2. Physician Restrictive Covenant--

Valley Medical Specialists v. Farber, 982 P.2d 1277 (Ariz. 1999).

Facts. Valley Medical Specialists (P) hired Farber (D), a doctor who performed brachytherapy, a procedure that involves radiating the inside of the lung that was used for lung cancer patients. Brachytherapy was a specialized procedure that could only be performed at hospitals that had certain equipment. D became a shareholder, officer, and director of P. D entered an employment agreement that contained a three-year restrictive covenant prohibiting D from competing with P within five miles of any of P's offices. D left P and started practicing medicine within the territory defined by the restrictive covenant. P sued for injunctive relief, liquidated damages, and other damages. The trial court declined to grant an injunction, finding the covenant was unenforceable because the duration was excessive, the geographic area covered was too great, and the restriction was not limited to pulmonology. The court of appeals reversed, finding that the covenant was reasonable. D appeals.

Issue. May a restrictive covenant in a doctor's employment contract be enforced if it lasts for three years and covers any practice of medicine within a large defined territory?

Held. No. Judgment reversed and case remanded.

♦ At common law, covenants not to compete were deemed restraints of trade and were not enforceable. Restraints that were ancillary, such as part of an employment or partnership agreement, were enforceable. However, restrictions on physicians were considered in light of the impact on public interests.

♦ The modern rule makes covenants not to compete invalid unless they protect a legitimate interest beyond the employer's desire to protect itself from competition. One legitimate interest is preventing the competitive use of proprietary information that the employee acquired in the course of employment.

♦ The covenant in this case resembles an employer-employee agreement. It is not like one involved in the sale of a business, where the buyer deserves protection against competition from the former owner.

♦ As at common law, restrictions involving physicians are subject to scrutiny because of the negative impact they may have on patient care. The American Bar Association prohibits restrictive covenants between attorneys. In like manner, the American Medical Association discourages covenants between doctors. Accordingly, such covenants must be strictly construed for reasonableness.

♦ To assess a restrictive covenant, the courts must consider the interests of the employer, employee, patients, and the public in general. As an employer, P does have a legitimate interest in retaining its customer base, but the personal relationship between doctor and patient affects the extent of that interest. D did not learn his skills from P. P's interests are therefore outweighed by other factors. In addition, the three-year term was excessive; anything over six months is unreasonable. Given the number of P's offices, the five-mile radius restriction covered more than 235 square miles and was unreasonable. Finally, the restriction on all types of practice was too broad, as well. Patient interests in seeing the doctor of their choice outweighs P's interests.

♦ The court of appeals revised the agreement to eliminate unreasonable provisions, but this application of the "blue pencil" rule was improper.

Comment. Public policy generally prohibits agreements in restraint of trade, in spite of the public interest that favors freedom to contract. The doctrine that a restraint may be valid if it is "ancillary" to a valid transaction is a means of accommodating both public policy interests.

---

3. **Surrogate Parenting--**

R.R. v. M.H. & another, 689 N.E.2d 790 (Mass. 1998).

Facts. R.R. (P) and his wife wanted to have children, but P's wife was infertile. They contacted the New England Surrogate Parenting Advisors ("NESPA") and paid NESPA a fee of $6,000 to help them find a woman willing to act as a surrogate mother. M.H. (D), a married mother of two, applied to NESPA to provide surrogacy services. After an interview with a psychologist, D signed a surrogate parenting agreement with P. The agreement provided that D would be inseminated with P's semen and that, on the birth of the child, P would have full legal parental rights. D would not lose her parental rights so long as she allowed P to have custody of the child. If she later sought custody, she would forfeit her contract rights and have to reimburse P the $10,000 surrogacy fee and associated costs. After D became pregnant and had accepted $3,000 of the fee, she changed her mind and wanted to keep the child. P sued for breach of contract. D's husband was added as a defendant. The trial court ordered D to give the child to P when it was discharged from the hospital, concluding that the surrogacy agreement was enforceable. The State Supreme Court assumed jurisdiction of D's appeal.

Issue. Is a surrogacy contract enforceable?

Held. No. Judgment reversed and case remanded.

♦ Some states deny enforcement of all surrogacy contracts, some deny enforcement only if the surrogate is paid, some merely provide that the contracts are not illegal, and some make unpaid surrogacy lawful. In *Matter of Baby M.*, 537 A.2d 1227 (N.J. 1988), the court invalidated a surrogacy contract because it required the mother to surrender her parental rights and allowed the father's wife to adopt the child. This violated the statute against paying money to adopt a child.

- State statutes permit surrogacy where the fertile wife is inseminated with sperm from an anonymous donor; in such cases, the mother and her husband are considered the lawful parents. No statute governs surrogacy where a child is born to a surrogate mother inseminated by the sperm of a fertile husband. Surrogate motherhood cannot be anonymous and therefore raises different issues than surrogate fatherhood.

- The policies reflected in the adoption statutes suggest that no private agreement about adoption or custody can be conclusive because a judge must make those decisions in the best interests of the child. In adoption, adoptive parents may not pay for receiving a child. Accordingly, a surrogate mother's agreement to surrender custody for pay should not be considered when deciding the custody of the child.

- By analogy to the adoption statute, D could not give consent to custody until the fourth day following the child's birth. Paying money to influence this decision makes any custody agreement void. The $10,000 fee cannot be deemed consideration for the services of carrying the child and giving birth because D had to forfeit that fee if she sought custody.

- A woman may contract to provide surrogate mother services so long as no compensation is paid for custody and she is not required to consent to grant custody before the child is born.

VIII. JUSTIFICATION FOR NONPERFORMANCE: MISTAKE, CHANGED CIRCUMSTANCES, AND CONTRACTUAL MODIFICATIONS

A. MISTAKE

1. **Mutual Mistake.** Where parties enter a contract while mutually mistaken concerning a *basic assumption of fact* on which the contract was made, and the mistake has a *material effect* on the agreed exchange, the contract is voidable by the party adversely affected. This rule applies unless the mistake goes to prediction or judgment, or unless there was an assumption of the risk of the mistake.

2. **Mistake as to Value.** Sometimes parties are mistaken as to the value of what they bargained for. When the mistake involves value alone, the courts generally do *not* permit one party to void the contract. This reflects in part the basic principle of contract law that courts do not inquire as to the wisdom of a particular bargain.

3. **Test for Granting Rescission--**

Lenawee County Board of Health v. Messerly, 331 N.W.2d 203 (Mich. 1982).

Facts. The Pickleses (D2) bought a three-unit apartment building from the Messerlys (D1) under a land purchase contract. Shortly thereafter, the Lenawee County Board of Health (P) condemned the property because D1's predecessor in title, Bloom, had installed an improper septic tank. P obtained an injunction against D1 and D2 prohibiting human habitation until the property conformed with the applicable sanitation code. The parties' contract provided that D2 had examined the property and agreed to accept it in its present condition. D2 refused to make payments, and D1 filed a cross-complaint for foreclosure, sale, and a deficiency judgment. D2 counterclaimed for rescission, alleging failure of consideration. The trial court found that D2 had no cause of action because there was no fraud or misrepresentation; D1 did not know of Bloom's conduct. In addition, D2 had purchased the property "as is." The court awarded judgment for D1. The court of appeals reversed on the ground that the parties had a mutual mistake as to a basic element of the contract. D1 appeals.

Issue. Is the value of a mistake a relevant consideration in determining whether rescission is available?

Held. Yes. Judgment reversed on equitable grounds.

◆ In contract law, a mistake is a belief that does not accord with the facts. The mistake must relate to a fact *in existence* when the contract is entered into; it cannot relate to a prediction. In this case, the parties were mistaken when they both believed that the property could be used as income-generating rental property, which was a mistake of fact.

◆ A remedy for mutual mistake of fact may be granted in the sound discretion of a court. The law has developed to the point that a mistake that affects the "essence of the consideration" may justify rescission, while one that involves the quality or value of the consideration may not. This is a confusing test. For example, in this case, the mistake directly affected the value of the consideration, but it also affected the essence of the consideration.

◆ The better approach is to permit rescission when the mistaken belief (i) relates to a *basic assumption* of the parties on which the contract is made, and (ii) *materially affects* the agreed performances of the parties.

◆ Although the mistake in this case satisfies the test, rescission is not appropriate in this case because D2 purchased the property under an "as is" clause pursuant to which D2 assumed the risk of the present condition of the property.

---

4.   **Unilateral Mistake Material Enough to Constitute Notice--**

Wil-Fred's, Inc. v. Metropolitan Sanitary District, 372 N.E.2d 946 (Ill. App. Ct. 1978).

Facts. Wil-Fred's, Inc. (P) submitted a sealed bid to the Metropolitan Sanitary District (D) to do rehabilitation work at one of D's water reclamation plants. P provided $100,000 as a security deposit. P was the low bidder at $882,600. D had estimated that the project would cost $1,257,000, and the second lowest bid was for $1,118,375. After the bids were opened, P had its sole subcontractor, Ciaglo, review its quotation. Ciaglo realized that it had made a substantial error of $150,000, based on its incorrect assumption that it could use heavy equipment to spread the granular fill. Ciaglo notified P that it would have to withdraw or file bankruptcy. With the withdrawal of Ciaglo, P could not do the work for the bid price. P attempted to withdraw. D rejected P's request and announced that P would be awarded the contract. P sought a preliminary injunction and rescission. The trial court granted rescission and ordered D to return P's deposit. D appeals.

Issue. May a unilateral mistake be grounds for rescission where the mistake is material enough to put the other party on notice of its existence?

Held. Yes. Judgment affirmed.

♦ The general rule does not allow rescission where only one party to a contract has made a mistake due to errors in judgment, but allows it for clerical or mathematical mistakes. A better approach focuses on the facts instead of the respective labels of "mistake of judgment" and "mistake of fact." This approach allows rescission if the facts satisfy the following requirements:

(i) The mistake relates to a material feature of the contract;

(ii) It occurred despite the exercise of reasonable care;

(iii) It is of such grave consequence that enforcement of the contract would be unconscionable; and

(iv) The other party can be placed in its original position.

♦ Ciaglo's mistake of $150,000 represents 17% of P's total bid. Under the circumstances, this is a material mistake. Given the discrepancy between P's bid and the next lowest bid, D should have been on notice that P's bid contained a material error.

♦ The consequences of Ciaglo's mistake were grave because P would either lose the $150,000 by performing, or the $100,000 security deposit P would forfeit by not performing, which would decrease P's bonding capacity by $2 to $3 million. Either alternative is a substantial hardship.

♦ D was not damaged seriously by P's withdrawal. P promptly notified D, before the contract had been awarded. D could easily have awarded the contract to the next lower bidder.

♦ The remaining issue is whether P exercised reasonable care. The fact of the mistake alone does not prove failure to use ordinary care. Ciaglo had several years of experience, including 12 previous projects with P, during which Ciaglo honored every quotation. Ciaglo conducted a reasonable investigation of the project before bidding. Its mistake was a mixed mistake of judgment and fact. P was justified in relying on Ciaglo and did not otherwise make mistakes in its bid.

B. CHANGED CIRCUMSTANCES: IMPOSSIBILITY, IMPRACTICABILITY, AND FRUSTRATION

1. **Introduction.** Performance of a contract may be excused if the performance has been rendered impossible or impracticable by the occurrence of an event whose nonoccurrence was a basic assumption on which the contract was made. Even where performance is not impracticable, if the purpose or value

of the contract has been destroyed or frustrated by the unforeseeable supervening event, performance may be excused.

a. **Supervening acts.** If the performance has become illegal due to a change in the law after the time of contracting, such as a change in zoning or an embargo, performance may be excused.

b. **Destruction of property.** Destruction of property, in the absence of fault by either party and apart from contractual provisions allocating the risk of destruction, can excuse performance, depending on the type of contract involved. In a repair contract, destruction of the premises to be repaired may excuse performance. In a construction contract, the destruction of the partially completed structure generally does not excuse performance. The destruction of a building to be leased would excuse performance. Destruction of goods identified when the contract was made excuses performance under U.C.C. section 2-613.

2. Economic Downturn--

Karl Wendt Farm Equipment Co. v. International Harvester Co., 931 F.2d 1112 (6th Cir. 1991).

Facts. Karl Wendt Farm Equipment Co. (P) had a dealership agreement with International Harvester Co. (D), a manufacturer of farm equipment. In light of a downturn in the market for farm equipment, D sustained large losses and sold its farm equipment business to J.I. Case Co. and Tenneco, Inc. ("Case") for over $400 million. When it purchased D's assets, Case did not acquire D's franchise network. Case granted dealerships to approximately two-thirds of D's former dealers, but P was in an area that conflicted with an existing Case dealer and so did not receive a Case dealership. P sued D for breach of the dealer agreement. D asserted the defense of impracticability of performance. The court submitted this defense to the jury, which found for D. The court also directed a verdict for P regarding D's other defenses. Both parties appeal.

Issue. Does a dramatic economic downturn constitute impracticability that excuses performance?

Held. No. Judgment reversed in part.

♦ Michigan courts have recognized the doctrine of impossibility and have expanded it to include impracticability, relying on the Restatement (Second) of Contracts, section 261. Under this approach, impracticability may arise from extreme and unreasonable difficulty, expense, injury, and loss.

♦ With respect to economic circumstances, impracticability requires more than a lack of profit, but it can include a shortage of raw materials due to war, embargo, or local crop failure. The key issue is whether the supervening event is such that the nonoccurrence of that event was a basic assumption on which both parties made the contract. The continuation of existing market conditions is ordinarily not such an assumption. Nor is the financial inability of one of the parties to perform.

♦ In this case, impracticability is an inappropriate defense because D was responding to market conditions. Neither that shift in the market nor D's financial problems fall within the meaning of impracticability such as to void a contract.

♦ D had other alternatives to unilateral termination of its contract with P, including sharing the proceeds of the sale with its dealers. To allow D to use the defense here would give D a windfall at P's expense.

♦ The trial court should have directed a verdict for P on D's defense of impracticability.

♦ The court properly directed a verdict for P based on D's frustration of purpose defense. Frustration of purpose is an equitable doctrine that apportions risk as the parties would have, had the necessity occurred to them. The frustrating event in this case was D selling its business. At the time of entering the contract, the parties would not have agreed to discharge D's obligations if it simply decided to sell its business.

Dissent. The jury, not an appellate court, should decide whether the alternatives D faced were feasible. Reasonable people could differ as to whether the facts in this case amounted to an event, the nonoccurrence of which was a basic assumption on which the contract was made.

---

3.   **Change in Law Leaves a Serviceable Use--**

Mel Frank Tool & Supply, Inc. v. Di-Chem Co., 580 N.W.2d 802 (Iowa 1998).

Facts. Di-Chem Co. (D) leased premises from Mel Frank Tool & Supply, Inc. (P), which D used to store hazardous chemicals. The lease required D to comply with all city ordinances and make no unlawful use of the premises. The lease also limited D's use of the premises to "storage and distribution." About a year after the lease started, city officials inspected the premises and determined that D's storage of hazardous chemicals violated a city ordinance that had been adopted after D began occupancy. D notified P that it would have to relocate. After D relocated and ceased paying rent, P sued for breach. D claimed impossibility as an affirmative defense. The trial court found for P. D appeals.

Issue. May a lessee be excused from performance when a city ordinance, adopted after the lease commences, prevents the lessee from continuing to use the property for its principal purpose, so long as there remains a serviceable use of the premises that is consistent with the use provision in the lease?

Held. No. Judgment affirmed.

♦ The trial court found that P did not know, and had no reason to believe, that D would store hazardous chemicals in the warehouse. P did not represent that the warehouse was suitable for any specific purpose. The lease merely provided that D could use the facilities for "storage and distribution."

♦ The Restatement (Second) of Contracts deals with impossibility of performance under the rubric of "impracticability of performance and frustration of purpose." Contract liability is strict liability and can be discharged only if one of the following events occurs:

   (i)   Circumstances make the obligor's performance impracticable;

   (ii)   Circumstances have so destroyed the value to the obligor of the other party's performance as to frustrate the obligor's own purpose in making the contract; or

   (iii) The obligor will not receive the agreed exchange for the obligee's duty to render that agreed exchange because of either impracticability or frustration.

♦ The key issue in a claim of impracticability and frustration is whether the nonoccurrence of the circumstances was a basic assumption on which the contract was made. The frustrated purpose must have been the principal purpose of the party in making the contract, and so clear that both parties understand that it is. The frustration must also be substantial; it must be so severe that it is not within the risks that the obligor assumed in making the contract.

♦ In this case, the city's ordinance did frustrate D's purpose, but D did not show at trial that all of its chemical inventory was hazardous. A fair inference from the evidence is that D stored nonhazardous material as well. Accordingly, D failed to show that its principal purpose in leasing the facility was substantially frustrated. D was free to continue storing and distributing nonhazardous chemicals.

Comment. Although D lost on these facts, supervening governmental action can be a valid reason for excusing performance. The key factor is whether the action renders the performance virtually worthless. In this case, D simply failed to prove that the prohibited uses were its principal purpose in making the contract.

C. MODIFICATION

1. **Introduction.** One exception to the rule that bargains are consideration is that a promise to perform an act that the promisor is already obligated to perform cannot be consideration. This rule, called the "legal duty" rule, applies even if the new promise is bargained for. A common application of this rule is in contract modifications. A related issue is the enforceability of an oral modification when the contract requires that all modifications be in writing.

   a. **Modification unenforceable.** A contract modification in which a party agrees to pay more for the same performance originally required is not enforceable as a general rule. Typically, such modifications are agreed to only when one of the parties threatens the other party in some way.

   b. **Modification enforceable.** A modification may be enforceable if it is based on an unanticipated change in circumstances and it is fair and equitable. The key is whether the new agreement varies in any way from the old, or whether it merely requires one party to increase the consideration it pays.

   c. **U.C.C. rule.** Under U.C.C. section 2-209(1), an agreement modifying a contract for the sale of goods is enforceable even if it is without consideration.

2. **Threat of Nonperformance--**

Alaska Packers' Association v. Domenico, 117 F. 99 (9th Cir. 1902).

Facts. In San Francisco, Domenico and other seamen (Ps) entered into a contract with the Alaska Packers' Association (D) to work as seamen and fishermen in a remote area of Alaska for $50 plus two cents per salmon caught. Ps sailed to Alaska but when they arrived at D's canning factory, they stopped work as a group and demanded $100 each. D's superintendent signed an agreement to pay the $100 because he could not get substitute workers. At the end of the season, D paid Ps according to the original contract. Ps sued in admiralty for the additional money. The court found for Ps. D appeals.

Issue. Is a contract to pay a higher salary than originally agreed, entered into under threat of nonperformance, enforceable?

Held. No. Judgment reversed.

♦ The supervisor's consent to Ps' demands was without consideration because it was based solely on Ps' agreement to render the exact services they were already under contract to render.

- A party who refuses to perform, thereby coercing the other party to promise to pay him more for doing what he was already legally bound to do, takes unjustifiable advantage of the other party. There is no consideration for the promise of the other party and it cannot be legally enforced. This is true even when the first party has completed his duty in reliance on the second contract.

Comment. Some courts find new consideration for a modified employment contract in the employee giving up his right to breach the first contract, for example, when the employee accepts a new contract with a higher salary rather than leaving the employment for a higher-paying job.

---

3. **Economic Duress to Force Modification--**

Kelsey-Hayes Co. v. Galtaco Redlaw Castings Corp., 749 F. Supp. 794 (E.D. Mich. 1990).

Facts. Kelsey-Hayes Co. (P) supplied brake assemblies to Ford and Chrysler. P purchased castings for the brake assemblies from Galtaco Redlaw Castings Corp. (D). P entered a three-year "requirements" contract with D, making D its sole supplier and specifying a fixed price for 1987, with scheduled price reductions in 1988 and 1989. In the spring of 1989, D's board decided to discontinue foundry operations due to large operating losses. Knowing that this shutdown would harm its customers, D offered to keep the foundry open for several months in return for a price increase of 30%. P signed an agreement in May 1989, but protested against the price increase. In June, D demanded an additional 30% price increase because all of its suppliers other than P had found other sources for castings. P accepted this price increase. P took 282 shipments from D and paid for the first 197. P still owed D $2 million, which reflected the amount of the price increase. P then sued for breach of contract. D defended on the ground that P's acceptance of the subsequent contracts constituted a waiver of any claim P had for breach of the prior agreement that was not expressly reserved, and P had not so reserved any claims. D moves for summary judgment.

Issue. Is a subsequent contract or modification valid when one party entered it in response to a threat by the other party to cease shipping under the original contract?

Held. No. Judgment for P.

- The general rule provides that entering a superseding, inconsistent agreement covering the same subject matter rescinds an earlier contract and acts as a waiver of any claim for breach of the earlier contract not expressly reserved. The exception is where the subsequent agreement is entered into under duress.

- At common law, to state a claim of duress, the proponent had to be subjected to the threat of an unlawful act in the nature of a tort or crime. Modern law has expanded the rule to make a contract voidable if a party's manifestation of assent is induced by an improper threat by another party that leaves the victim no reasonable alternative.

♦   In this case, D's threat to breach its contract and go out of business unless P agreed to the substantial price increases left P no reasonable alternative. P sought an alternative supplier but was unsuccessful. If P stopped shipping its brake assemblies, its customers would have to shut down their entire production lines, which would subject P to large monetary damages.

♦   P has demonstrated sufficient evidence to state a claim of economic duress. While P signed the subsequent agreement, it did so under vigorous protest. Even though P did not reserve its right to sue under the 1987 contract, D was on notice that P considered itself under duress when it signed the subsequent agreements.

---

4.   Reliance on Oral Modification--

Brookside Farms v. Mama Rizzo's, Inc., 873 F. Supp. 1029 (S.D. Tex. 1995).

Facts. Brookside Farms (P) entered a contract to supply all of the requirements of Mama Rizzo's, Inc. (D) for fresh basil leaves. D agreed to purchase a minimum of 91,000 pounds of leaves in one year. P was to deliver leaves daily. The price was specified, although it varied with the seasons. D asked P to remove additional parts of the stems of the leaves, which was not required under the original contract. P verbally agreed to do this for an additional $0.50 per pound. Although the original contract prohibited oral modifications, the new price terms were reflected on the parties' purchase orders, invoices, and payments. D ceased ordering leaves for about two months, and P responded by reducing its purchases from its own suppliers. When D resumed orders, P had to pay a higher price. D agreed to pay a higher price. After one of D's checks was dishonored for insufficient funds, P sued for the amount due and also claimed that D breached the contract by not accepting the minimum amount under the contract. D claimed that P breached by raising prices without having a written modification. The parties moved for summary judgment.

Issue. Where a contract requires that all modifications must be in writing, may an oral modification still be enforceable if the parties acted in reliance on it?

Held. Yes. P's motion is granted in part; D's motion is denied.

♦   When D orally agreed to the price increase, its vice president agreed to note the price change on D's copy of the original contract. The parties reflected the price increases in their documentation.

♦ The contract falls within the Statute of Frauds, and, generally, an oral agreement that materially modifies a written agreement within the Statute of Frauds is not enforceable. There is a promissory estoppel exception where one party relies on the oral promise of the other to put an oral agreement in writing. There is a second exception under U.C.C. section 2-201(c)(3) which states that a contract that does not satisfy the Statute of Frauds is enforceable with respect to goods for which payment has been made and accepted or which have been received and accepted.

♦ In this case, the oral modification of the contract is valid on both estoppel and statutory grounds. D induced P's reliance on the oral price modification. The parties' subsequent conduct satisfies the statutory requirement. If D asserts its right to demand full performance of the written contract, then P could also assert its right to ship without removing the stem parts. More importantly, though, the parties have created a private Statute of Frauds, under which they entered an effective agreement with respect to the leaves P shipped and D received and accepted.

♦ P claims that D is also liable for not accepting the minimum amount of basil called for in the contract. D claims it was relieved of this obligation by P's demand for higher prices than the contract specified. Since P's price increases were legally justified, D's defense fails and D is liable for a material breach of its obligation to purchase the minimum quantity.

Comment. Under U.C.C. section 2-209(2), parties to a contract can use a "no-oral-modification" clause to create a "private Statute of Frauds" that governs modifications. They could require a writing even where the Statute of Frauds would not. However, even a no-oral-modification clause can be waived by oral agreement or by a combination of words and conduct that demonstrate a different agreement. In this case, the court also held that the parties orally waived their no-waiver clause. Despite parties' efforts to make sure that only their written contract is binding, courts tend to look at the implied obligations of good faith and fair dealing, estoppel, and the possibility of fraud and nondisclosure when they determine what agreements to enforce.

IX. RIGHTS AND DUTIES OF THIRD PARTIES

A. RIGHTS OF THIRD PARTIES AS CONTRACT BENEFICIARIES

1. **Introduction.** Two persons may validly contract for a performance to be rendered to a third person. The question normally raised is whether that third person, who was not a party to the contract and gave no consideration for the promise, may enforce the promise made for his benefit.

   a. **Example.** For example, if A offers to paint B's house if B will promise to pay $1,000 to C, can C enforce B's promise (here, B is the promisor, A is the promisee, and C is the third-party beneficiary)?

   b. **Common law.** The common law rule was that the third party could not enforce the promise since he was not in privity of contract.

   c. **Modern law.** The modern rule is that the third party may normally enforce the promise made for his benefit.

2. **Classification of Beneficiaries.** If a contract was made for the benefit of a third party, that party's status as a beneficiary must be determined.

   a. **Intended vs. incidental beneficiaries.** To enforce the promise, the third party involved must be more than a mere "incidental beneficiary." [*See* Restatement (Second) §302]

      1) **The test.** Unless the contract is made primarily for the benefit of the third party, the third party is only an incidental beneficiary and cannot enforce the contract. Therefore, to be enforceable by the third party, it must appear that a major purpose of the contract (although not the only one) was to benefit the third party.

      2) **Factors considered.** In making the determination as to whether the third party is an intended beneficiary or is merely an incidental beneficiary, the courts attempt to determine the intent of the promisee (*i.e.*, did the promisee intend the promisor's performance to be rendered to the third party?). The following factors are looked at:

         a) Is performance to be rendered directly to the third party?

         b) Do express provisions of the contract purport to create rights in third parties?

      c)   Are third parties specifically named in the contract?

      d)   Is there a close relationship between the promisee and the third parties?

b.   Creditor and donee beneficiaries.

    1)   The test. The test is whether the promisee intended to confer a gift on a third party (donee beneficiary) or to discharge some obligation owed to the third party (creditor beneficiary).

    2)   Creditor beneficiaries. If the promisee's primary intent was to discharge a duty he owed to the third party, the third party is a creditor beneficiary. The older view was that there actually had to be a debt owing to the third party. The modern view is that the test is whether the promisee intended to satisfy an obligation that he believed was owed to the third party (even though there might not actually be such a debt).

    3)   Donee beneficiaries. If the promisee's primary intent in contracting was to confer a gift on the third party (*i.e.*, to confer some performance neither due, asserted, nor supposed to be due from the promisee to the third party), the third party is a donee beneficiary.

    4)   Restatement (Second) position. The Restatement (Second) substitutes the term "intended beneficiary" for both creditor and donee beneficiary, the purpose being to eliminate the distinctions that currently exist between the vesting of rights for creditor and donee beneficiaries. But most states still recognize a difference and use the old terminology.

3.   Intent to Benefit Third Party--

Vogan v. Hayes Appraisal Associates, Inc., 588 N.W.2d 420 (Iowa 1999).

Facts. The Vogans (Ps) purchased a lot for $66,000 and obtained a $170,000 construction loan from MidAmerica Savings Bank. MidAmerica hired Hayes Appraisal Associates, Inc. (D) to monitor the progress of Ps' home construction project. D appraised the future home at a value of $250,000. MidAmerica disbursed progress payments to the contractor based on reports provided by D. After MidAmerica had disbursed all but $2,000 of the loan, the contractor determined that it would take another $70,000 to complete the home due to cost overruns. Ps took out a second mortgage to complete the home. D provided varying estimates of completion before the contractor defaulted, leaving an estimated $60,000 worth of work left to do. Ps defaulted on the mortgage and MidAmerica sued to foreclose. Ps counterclaimed based on improper authorization of disbursements. Those parties settled. Ps then sued D, claiming they were third-party beneficiaries of D's contract with MidAmerica. The jury found for Ps. The court of appeals reversed. Ps appeal.

Issue. May a third-party beneficiary arise when a contract manifests an intent to benefit a third party, even if the intent is not to benefit the third party directly?

Held. Yes. Judgment reversed.

♦   A beneficiary of a promise is an intended beneficiary if recognition of that status is appropriate to effectuate the intention of the parties and the circumstances indicate that the promisee intends to give the beneficiary the benefit of the promised performance. In this case, MidAmerica was the promisee and D was the promisor.

♦   D's promised performance was to be of pecuniary benefit to Ps, and the contract language gives D reason to know that MidAmerica contemplated that benefit as a motivating cause for entering the contract. MidAmerica obtained the periodic progress reports from D in part to provide Ps some protection for their investment. Accordingly, Ps were third-party beneficiaries of the contract between D and MidAmerica.

♦   The court of appeals concluded that D did not damage Ps because MidAmerica had already disbursed most of the $170,000 before receiving D's erroneous progress reports. However, MidAmerica did rely on D's faulty report before disbursing the additional money raised by Ps; these funds would not have been disbursed had D's report been accurate.

♦   When D contracted with MidAmerica, the type of damage suffered by Ps was within D's contemplation, so recovery here does not violate *Hadley v. Baxendale*, 9 Exch. 341 (1854).

---

4.   **Tenants as Third-Party Beneficiaries--**

Zigas v. Superior Court, 174 Cal. Rptr. 806 (Cal. Ct. App. 1981), *cert. denied*, 455 U.S. 943 (1982).

Facts. Zigas and other tenants (Ps) paid rent to the landlords of an apartment building that was financed with a federally insured mortgage. Ps brought a class action against the landlords, claiming that they were charging higher rent than was allowed under the federal financing agreement with the Department of Housing and Urban Development ("HUD"). The landlords were required to file a maximum rental schedule with HUD.

Ps sued in part as third-party beneficiaries. The Superior Court (D) sustained the land-lords' demurrers. Ps petitioned for a writ of mandate.

Issue. Do tenants have standing as third-party beneficiaries to enforce a maximum rent schedule that is part of an agreement between their landlords and the federal government?

Held. Yes. Writ granted and case remanded.

♦ Ps are not alleging a federal cause of action, but are relying on state contract law as third-party beneficiaries. Under *Shell v. Schmidt*, 272 P.2d 82 (Cal. App. 1954), private parties may be third-party beneficiaries where a government agency is a party to the contract, and the private parties are in the class intended to be protected by that contract.

♦ In this case, the agreement between the landlords and HUD could only benefit Ps because it required HUD to approve rent increases. The statute on which the financing agreement was based stated that it was intended to facilitate reasonable rents.

♦ However, in *Martinez v. Socoma Cos.*, 521 P.2d 841 (Cal. 1974), the court limited *Shell* to require that the contract with the government manifest an intention that the promisor shall compensate members of the public for injurious consequences of failing to perform. This means that, absent such an intent in the HUD agreement, Ps would only be incidental beneficiaries without standing.

♦ In *Martinez*, the government itself was to receive a refund if Socoma failed to perform; here, as in Shell, the government itself would not lose money if the landlords charged excess rent. In *Martinez*, the contracts were not designed to benefit individuals, but in this case, the HUD agreements were designed to provide moderately priced rental housing. The HUD agreement's provisions also demonstrate an intent to make Ps direct beneficiaries.

♦ Ps claim that the landlords have retained over $2 million in excess rent. This money was taken from Ps, not from the government, and Ps should have standing to recover it.

B. ASSIGNMENT AND DELEGATION OF CONTRACTUAL RIGHTS AND DUTIES

1. **Introduction.** Often one or both of the original contracting parties seeks to transfer to another some right arising from the contract or some duty of per-

formance created thereby. Assignment or delegation occurs where the original contract did not contemplate performance to a third party (unlike third-party beneficiary contracts) but where one of the parties, subsequent to the original contract, seeks to achieve this result.

a. **Nature of an assignment.** An assignment is the transfer of a contractual right, which operates to extinguish the right in the transferor (the *assignor*), and to set it up exclusively in the transferee (the *assignee*). [Restatement (Second) §317]

   1) **Effect.** The effective assignment of a contractual right operates to give the assignee a direct right against the obligor under the contract.

   2) **Real party in interest.** Although the early common law rule was to the contrary, every jurisdiction today recognizes that an assignee is the real owner of the right transferred to him, and that he alone may enforce the contract against the obligor or debtor. In other words, the assignee is the real party in interest insofar as that right is concerned, and he may sue directly on the contract in his own name, without joining the assignor.

   3) **Partial assignments.** Rights under a contract may be transferred to one assignee or divided up among several. Alternatively, only some of the rights under a contract may be assigned and the balance retained by the assignor.

b. **Nature of a delegation.** A delegation of contractual duties is really not a transfer of such duties, because the delegating party always remains liable for performance thereof if the party to whom the duties are delegated fails to perform. Rather, a delegation is simply an appointment by the obligor under the contract to another to perform the obligor's contractual duties. The delegating party (obligor) is called the "delegant," while the party to whom the duties are delegated is the "delegatee." [Restatement (Second) §318]

   1) **Promise to assume duties.** As part of a delegation of duties, the delegatee may expressly or impliedly promise the delegant that he will perform the duties owed by the delegant to the other party to the contract. This is a typical assumption agreement; *i.e.*, a third-party creditor beneficiary contract, which gives the other party (the obligee) a right of action directly against the delegatee.

   2) **Implied assumption of duties?** There is no question but that the rights under a contract can be assigned without any delegation of duties, or, conversely, that duties can be delegated but rights retained. However, the more frequent cases involve attempts to as-

sign rights and delegate duties at the same time. If this intent is clearly manifest, there are no problems. Often, however, there is simply an "assignment of the contract," with no express agreement by the "assignee" to perform obligations still due from the assignor. The question is whether the courts should infer the assignee's obligation to perform from the fact that he has accepted benefits under the contract. There is no easy answer to this question, as the courts are widely split on the issue.

2. **Impact of the U.C.C.** In many instances, the common law rules have been drastically altered by the U.C.C. The common law rules are important today primarily as a background for the U.C.C. provisions, and because they govern those few types of assignments that are expressly excluded from the U.C.C. *(e.g.,* assignments of insurance benefits, wages, interests in real estate, bank accounts; assignments as part of a sale of an entire business; etc.).

3. **Assignment Enforceable Despite Attempt to Revoke--**

Herzog v. Irace, 594 A.2d 1106 (Me. 1991).

Facts. Jones was injured in a motorcycle accident and retained attorneys Irace and Lowry (Ds) to represent him. Before recovering any money for the accident, Jones was injured again. Herzog (P) performed surgery to repair Jones's new injuries. Jones could not pay for the surgery but gave P a letter stating that he requested that payment be made directly to P from the settlement of the motorcycle accident. P notified Ds that Jones had assigned him the benefits from the motorcycle accident and was told by Ds' employee that the assignment was sufficient to allow Ds to pay P's bills when recovery was made. Jones received a $20,000 settlement for the motorcycle accident. He then instructed Ds not to pay P directly but that he would pay P. Ds notified P that Jones had revoked his permission to have Ds pay P and they paid Jones the money. Jones gave P a check, but it was returned for insufficient funds and P was never paid. P sued Ds. The court found for P. Ds appeal.

Issue. May a party who makes a valid assignment later revoke the assignment?

Held. No. Judgment affirmed.

- ♦ Once a valid assignment is made, and the obligor has notice of the assignment, the fund is impressed with a trust, and the obligor holds the fund not for the original creditor, the assignor, but for the substituted creditor, the assignee. At this point, the obligor cannot pay the amount assigned either to the assignor or to his other creditors. If he does so, he is personally liable to the assignee.

- ♦ Jones's letter to P constituted a proper assignment of his future right to proceeds from pending litigation. P received a preference over Jones's other creditors through the assignment. Ds were therefore obligated to pay P, regardless of Jones's subsequent attempt to revoke the assignment.

♦ Ds claim that they were obligated by the rules of ethics to pay the proceeds as directed by Jones. However, the ethical rules do not affect a client's power to assign his right to proceeds from a pending lawsuit to third parties, and a valid assignment must be honored by the attorney in disbursing the funds on the client's behalf. Ds had no ethical obligation to honor a client's instruction to disregard a valid assignment.

---

4. **Assignability of Rights and Delegability of Duties.**

   a. **General rule of assignability.** The general rule is that all contract rights are assignable. Subject to the exceptions noted below, there is a strong public policy favoring the free flow of commerce and the assignability of commercial obligations.

   b. **Exceptions—nonassignable rights.** The few situations in which contract rights are not assignable involve specific policy factors that outweigh the general policy of free alienation of contract rights. As stated in Restatement (Second) section 317, a right may not be assigned where it would "materially change the duty of the obligor, or materially increase the burden or risk imposed on him by his contract, or materially impair his chance of obtaining return performance, or materially reduce its value to him."

      1) **Assignment altering the obligor's duty.**

         a) **Personal service contracts.** Rights may not be assigned if the effect would be to require the obligor to perform personal services to someone other than the original obligee. The performance of personal services to anyone other than the original obligee could materially change the nature of the obligor's duties—*e.g.*, painting C's picture may prove a harder task than painting A's. Wherever such services are involved, the law implies that the personal relationship between the obligor and obligee will be maintained; thus, the obligee cannot transfer his rights to another.

         b) **Requirement and output contracts.** Rights under requirement and output contracts generally are not assignable since the assignee might have far greater or lesser "output" or far different "requirements" than the assignor.

         c) **Change in terms.** Even if the assignment will not materially affect the obligor's duty, it cannot alter essential terms of the contract, such as time or place of delivery. Thus, the assignee must accept delivery at the assignor's place of business if that is what the contract calls for.

2) **Assignment varying the risk assumed by the obligor.** No assignment may be made if it would require the obligor to assume a risk materially different from that originally contemplated.

    a) **Insurance.** Since the risk assumed in insuring a particular person necessarily differs from that assumed in insuring any other, the right to be insured under a specific policy is generally not assignable.

    b) **Credit.** Where personal credit is involved, any substitution of debtors varies the risk, and no assignment is permitted.

c. **Contractual prohibition against assignment.** Traditionally, such provisions were enforced. However, Restatement (Second) section 322 adopts a strong rule of construction against such provisions and U.C.C. section 9-406(d) renders such provisions ineffective to prevent assignment of most types of rights to payment.

d. **General rule of delegation.** Any contractual duty may be delegated to another, unless the obligee has a substantial interest in having the original obligor perform personally. Thus, except in those cases where performance by a delegatee would vary materially from the performance promised by the obligor, the duty may be performed by some agent or servant of the original promisor (or an independent third party) without constituting a breach of contract. [*See* Restatement (Second) §318; U.C.C. §2-210(1)]

1) **Effect of valid delegation of duties.** A valid delegation of duties does not excuse the delegating party (delegant) from his duty to perform. It merely places the primary responsibility to perform on the delegatee (who becomes the principal debtor). The delegant becomes secondarily liable (as a surety) for performance of the duty promised.

    a) **Compare—assignment of rights.** Contrast this with the effect of a valid assignment of rights, which operates to extinguish the rights in the assignor and sets them up entirely in the assignee. This distinction is critical in the frequent cases which involve both an assignment of rights and a delegation of duties. In such cases, the assignor-delegant is cut off from any benefits under the contract, but still remains potentially liable for its performance.

    b) **U.C.C.—right of obligee to demand assurance.** In contracts for the sale of goods, the very fact that duties of performance have been delegated entitles the obligee to demand assurances of performance from the delegatee. [*See* U.C.C. §2-210(5)]

2) Rights and liabilities of the parties following valid delegation of duties.

a) Where delegatee has expressly assumed the duty. If the delegation arises out of a transaction in which the obligor-delegant bargained to have someone take over his obligation, he may have extracted an express promise to perform from the delegatee. For example, A sells his business to B, and as part of the transaction obtains B's promise to pay off all the existing creditors of the business (to whom A was personally liable). Where the delegatee has expressly assumed the delegant's obligations to the other contracting party, a ***third-party creditor beneficiary contract*** exists—*i.e.*, the typical "assumption agreement."

(1) Thus, in the event of nonperformance, the delegatee is directly liable to the obligee (creditor beneficiary).

(2) Moreover, the delegatee is also liable to the delegant (original obligor) for breach of the assumption agreement. The delegant (now surety for the obligation) has the right to an equitable decree of specific performance to compel the delegatee (as principal debtor) to perform. Or, in the event that the obligor-delegant has been forced to perform himself, he can hold the delegatee liable in damages for breach of contract.

b) Where delegatee has not expressly assumed the duty. If the delegation is made apart from any assignment of rights under the contract, and there is no express assumption of contract duties, the delegatee's only liability is to the delegant.

5. Prevention of Assignment to a Competitor--

Sally Beauty Co. v. Nexxus Products Co., 801 F.2d 1001 (7th Cir. 1986).

Facts. Best Barber & Beauty Supply Co. became the exclusive Texas distributor of hair care products made by Nexxus Products Co. (D). Sally Beauty Co. (P) purchased Best, and D cancelled the distribution agreement. P was itself owned by a hair care products manufacturer that competed with D. P sued for breach, but D claimed the contract was not assignable. The district court granted summary judgment for D on the ground that the contract was one for personal services. P appeals.

Issue. May a party to an otherwise assignable contract prevent assignment to its competitor?

Held. Yes. Judgment affirmed.

- The sales aspect of the distribution contract was significant enough that the U.C.C. applies to this case. The trial court erred in holding the contract was for personal services instead of for the sale of goods.

- Under U.C.C. section 2-210, delegation of performance and assignability are normally permitted. However, the other party to a contract may prevent assignment if it has a "substantial interest" in having the original promisor perform the contractual duties. This case involves the delegation of Best's duty of performance. D did not accept P's substituted performance; D had promised to refrain from supplying other distributors in Texas in return for Best's promise to use its best efforts to sell D's goods. D should not be required to accept P's best efforts when those efforts are subject to the control of one of D's competitors.

- Unlike Best, P is a subsidiary of one of D's direct competitors. P's competitive position gives D a substantial interest in not having P perform the exclusive distribution duties. D may not be forced to assume the risk of an unfavorable outcome in the event the interests of P's parent company conflict with those of D. Thus the duty of performance under an exclusive distributorship may not be delegated to a competitor in the marketplace.

Dissent. It is not uncommon in business for companies to do business with competitors. P carried hair care supplies made by many different companies that compete with P's parent as much as D does. It is not very likely that P's acquisition of Best would hurt D. The other competitors would not continue to allow P to distribute their products if P favored its parent's products. If P failed to use its best efforts, it would be liable in damages to D for breach.

X. CONSEQUENCES OF NONPERFORMANCE: EXPRESS CONDITIONS, MATERIAL BREACH, AND ANTICIPATORY REPUDIATION

A. EXPRESS CONDITIONS

1. **Introduction.** A condition is a fact or event, the occurrence or nonoccurrence of which creates or extinguishes a duty to perform on the part of the promisor. It differs from a promise; a condition typically qualifies a promise in some way. In some cases, it is difficult to determine whether a specific contractual provision was intended as a promise or as a condition.

   a. **Express and implied conditions.** Conditions may be classified as express or implied (constructive). An express condition is one explicitly set forth in the contract. A contract may include as many or as few conditions as desired, subject to limitations of statute and public policy. An implied condition is one that the parties would probably have agreed to if they had thought about the subject. The courts generally infer whatever conditions are inherent in the promises given that are necessary to the performance of the contract, such as the implied condition of good faith performance.

   b. **Legal effect of conditions.** If a promise to perform is conditional, there can be no breach of the promise until the duty to perform is absolute. This requires the occurrence of the conditions attached to the duty.

2. **Conditions Precedent and Subsequent.** Conditions can either create or extinguish an otherwise absolute duty to perform, depending on when the condition occurs.

   a. **Conditions precedent.** A condition precedent is one that must occur in order to create an absolute duty to perform; that is, there is no duty owed until the conditional fact or event occurs.

      1) **Example.** If A promises to pay B $1,000 if B paints A's house by June 1, painting the house by June 1 is a condition precedent to A's absolute duty to pay B $1,000. If B completes the painting by June 1, A's promise to pay becomes absolute and unconditional.

However, if B does not complete the painting, there is no breach of contract by anyone.

2) **Condition and promise.** A condition may also be a promise. In the above example, A may promise to pay B $1,000 and B may promise A to paint the house by June 1. The promise to paint the house by June 1 is now both a promise and a condition precedent to A's duty to pay B $1,000. Now, if B fails to paint the house by June 1, he has breached the contract and A may collect damages. There is also a failure of a condition precedent to A's duty to pay, so A's duty to pay never arises.

b. **Conditions subsequent.** A condition subsequent is one in which the occurrence of the condition extinguishes a previously absolute duty to perform.

1) **Example.** If A agrees to work for B for one year unless A is drafted into military service, A is under an absolute duty to perform, unless during the term he is called into service (which would extinguish his duty to perform).

2) **Contract construction.** Conditions subsequent are rare and are disfavored by the courts. Many provisions that appear to be conditions subsequent are interpreted as conditions precedent. For example, if an insurance policy provides that a claim will be paid only if submitted within 90 days of the accident, this appears to be a condition subsequent, but courts hold that it is a condition precedent; the insurer has no duty to pay unless the condition of submitting the claim within 90 days is first satisfied.

c. **Conditions concurrent.** Conditions concurrent are mutually dependent performances that are capable of nearly simultaneous performance by the parties. They occur when the parties to the contract are bound to render performance at the same time. For example, in a contract for the sale of goods, A covenants to deliver widgets on June 1 and B promises to pay for them. Each promise (by A and B) is also a condition of the other's performance, and since they are mutually dependent and capable of simultaneous performance, they are conditions concurrent.

3. **Contract Interpretation.** Nonoccurrence of a condition is not a breach of contract, but failure to perform a promise is a breach. Therefore, a critical aspect of contract interpretation is determining whether a provision is a condition or a promise.

a. **The parties' intent.** The intent of the parties determines whether a particular provision is a promise or a condition, but in many instances, the contract itself is ambiguous.

b. Factors considered.

1) **Words used.** Words such as "provided," "if," "when," and so forth usually indicate that a condition is involved. Words such as "promise," "agreed," etc., generally indicate that a promise was intended.

2) **Custom.** Common usage or understanding may be determinative.

3) **Protection of expectancies of the parties.** Doubtful provisions are normally construed as promises rather than conditions.[*See* Restatement (Second) §227] The rationale is that this operates to uphold and make enforceable the contract and allow damages for nonperformance.

4. **Excuse.** A conditional duty may become absolute by occurrence of the condition or by excuse of the condition. The rules governing excuse of conditions operate to change or modify the express provisions of the contract by eliminating some condition upon which the parties had agreed.

   a. **Prevention.** A condition will be legally excused if the party whose duty was conditional wrongfully prevents or hinders the occurrence of the condition.

   b. **Forfeiture.** If the nonoccurrence of a condition would cause disproportionate forfeiture, the nonoccurrence may be excused unless the condition was a material part of the agreed exchange.

   c. **Impracticability.** Impracticability may excuse nonoccurrence if the condition is not material and forfeiture would result by not excusing the nonoccurrence.

   d. **Separate promise.** A party's promise to perform a duty in spite of the nonoccurrence of a condition is generally binding. [*See* Restatement (Second) §841]

5. **Strict Enforcement of Express Condition Precedent--**

Oppenheimer & Co. v. Oppenheim, Appel, Dixon & Co., 660 N.E.2d 415 (N.Y. 1995).

Facts. Oppenheimer & Co. (P) moved from the 33rd floor of One New York Plaza to the World Financial Center. Its new landlord guaranteed to pay P's rental payments on the three remaining years of its 33rd floor lease if P could not sublease that space. Oppenheim, Appel, Dixon & Co. (D) already leased the 29th floor of One New York Plaza and agreed to sublease the 33rd floor from P, provided that P first obtain the prime landlord's written notice of confirmation of D's suitability, as well as of consent to specified "tenant work" by a certain date. This date was extended by agreement to February 25, 1987. P did provide the prime landlord's written consent to D's suitability, but only told D by telephone on February 25th that the landlord had agreed to the tenant work. On February 26th, D notified P that the sublease was invalid because P had not delivered the prime landlord's written consent as required. P did eventually deliver the written consent to D on March 20. P sued for breach of contract, claiming that D waived the condition or was estopped from insisting on physical delivery of consent by February 25th by virtue of its previous extensions of the deadline. The trial court submitted the question of substantial performance to the jury. The jury awarded P damages of $1.2 million. The court granted D's motion for judgment notwithstanding the verdict on the ground that substantial performance was not applicable. The appellate division reversed. D appeals.

Issue. May a party insist on exact compliance with a specific condition precedent?

Held. Yes. Judgment reversed.

♦ A condition precedent is an act or event that must occur before a duty to perform a promise in the agreement arises, although the very formation of a contract may also be contingent on the occurrence of a condition precedent. Such a condition may be express or implied.

♦ Generally, an express condition precedent must be literally performed. An implied or constructive condition usually arises from the language of promise and may be satisfied by substantial compliance. Courts favor contract interpretations that lead to a constructive condition over an express condition because of the risk of forfeiture, but where the language is clear, the courts must give effect to an express condition.

♦ In this case, the contract language was clear, leaving no doubt about the parties' intent. P did not show that the nonoccurrence of the condition should be excused because of forfeiture. P simply claims that D waived or should be estopped from enforcing the condition and that, at any rate, it substantially complied.

♦ The doctrine of substantial compliance is inapplicable to express conditions. P could only obtain excuse of the nonoccurrence of the condition to avoid forfeiture. However, P has not suffered any forfeiture or conferred any benefit upon D.

6.   **Relief from Forfeiture--**

J.N.A. Realty Corp. v. Cross Bay Chelsea, Inc., 366 N.E.2d 1313 (N.Y.

1977).

Facts. J.N.A. Realty Corporation (P) leased a building to Palermo and Vascellero for a period of 10 years, with an option to renew, provided that written notice be given six months prior to the expiration of the term. Palermo and Vascellero assigned the lease to Foro Romano Corporation, which operated a restaurant on the premises. Foro later sold the restaurant and assigned the lease to Cross Bay Chelsea, Inc. (D). As a condition of the sale, Foro was required to obtain a modification of the option to renew so that D would have the right to renew the lease for an additional term of 24 years. P consented. Either through negligence or inadvertence, D did not send its notice to renew within the prescribed period. After the option had thus lapsed, P demanded that D vacate the premises. P commenced this proceeding to recover possession of the premises, claiming that the lease had expired. D sought relief in equity from the harsh results of a forfeiture. The trial court found D to be negligent in failing to renew within the time prescribed. D appeals.

Issue. May a court of equity grant a tenant relief from forfeiture where the forfeiture would result from the tenant's own neglect or inadvertence in failing to renew a lease within the prescribed time limit?

Held. Yes. Judgment reversed and new trial granted.

♦   Equity may grant relief from forfeiture even where that forfeiture would result from the tenant's own negligence or inadvertence. This is true although the tenant has no legal interest in the renewal period until the required notice is given. An equitable interest is recognized and protected against forfeiture in cases where the tenant has, in good faith, made substantial improvements with the intention of renewing the lease and the landlord would not be harmed by the delay in giving notice.

♦   D invested a considerable amount in improvements on the premises. If the location were lost, D would suffer the loss of much customer goodwill. If a forfeiture were allowed in such a case, the gravity of the loss would be out of all proportion to the gravity of the fault. Thus, absent prejudice to P, D is entitled to equitable relief.

Dissent. This is a situation where the only excuse for the commercial tenant's dilatory failure to exercise its option to renew is sheer carelessness. The tenant seeks to keep his old bargain and the landlord wants to obtain a higher return. It is not within the province of the courts to determine which of the profit-seeking parties should prevail as a matter of morals. It does not suffice that the tenant may suffer economic detriment and that the delay in giving notice caused the landlord no prejudice. A commercial lessee should not be heard to complain that through its own carelessness a valuable asset was lost, any more than a landlord should be allowed to complain of economic detriment to him in agreeing to an improvident option to renew.

B. MATERIAL BREACH

1. **Introduction.** Any breach of contract can give rise to an immediate cause of action for damages, but it may not excuse the nonbreaching party's duty of performance. To excuse a duty of performance, the breach must be "material" as opposed to "minor." There are several factors the courts consider to determine whether a breach is material or minor:

   a. The extent of the breaching party's performance. An early breach is more likely to be considered a material breach than a later breach.

   b. The nature of the breach; *i.e.*, whether the breach was willful, negligent, or innocent. A willful breach is more likely to be held material.

   c. The degree of uncertainty whether the breaching party will perform the remainder of the contract.

   d. The extent to which the nonbreaching party will obtain (or has obtained) the benefit of the bargain, despite the breach.

   e. The adequacy of contract remedies to compensate the nonbreaching party for defective or incomplete performance.

   f. The degree of hardship suffered by the breaching party if the breach is deemed material.

2. **Substantial Performance.** Where A substantially performs a condition in his contract with B, A may enforce the contract (the constructive condition of his complete performance being excused). B may, however, collect damages for the defective performance by A.

3. **Substitution of Materials--**

Jacob & Youngs, Inc. v. Kent, 129 N.E. 889 (N.Y. 1921).

Facts. Jacob & Youngs, Inc. (P) built Kent (D) a house, using pipe substantially similar to but different from the "Reading" pipe required by the contract. P asked for the final payment (nine months after D occupied the house), but D's architect refused to give the required certificate because the wrong pipe had been installed. Great expense would have been required to change the pipe, and the value of the house was not reduced by the substitution. P sued for the payment. The breach was not willful by P. P was not allowed to show the identical quality, appearance, and cost of the installed pipe. Verdict was directed for D. The appellate court reversed. D appeals.

Issue. If complete performance in accord with contract specifications is a condition precedent to payment, and if substantial performance has been rendered, will a minor failure to perform be excused?

Held. Yes. Judgment affirmed.

♦   If the omission is trivial and not willful, it will be excused and damages for the minor breach of condition will be allowed rather than holding that there is a breach of condition forfeiting the entire contract.

♦   Damages for D should be measured by the loss in value (rather than cost of replacing the pipe).

Dissent. D had the right to contract for the Reading pipe, and P offers no explanation as to why it did not install it. P was grossly negligent in installing the wrong pipe and should therefore not recover.

---

4.   Payment of One-Third of Purchase Price--

Sackett v. Spindler, 56 Cal. Rptr. 435 (Cal. Ct. App. 1967).

Facts. Spindler (D) was the majority owner of S & S Newspapers. D was also the publisher, editor, and general manager of the company's newspaper. D contracted to sell all of the outstanding stock to Sackett (P) for $85,000, payable over July and August. P made the first two payments, but his final August 10 payment for the balance of $59,200 was returned for insufficient funds. In the meantime, D had purchased the stock owned by the minority shareholders and delivered all but 454 shares to P's lawyers to hold in escrow. When P's check bounced, D reclaimed the stock certificates. The parties agreed to two extensions for the final payment in September, but P missed both of these and ultimately failed to provide the final payment. P did provide $3,944.26 for working capital, however. In the meantime, D had mortgaged other property to help finance the newspaper. On October 5, D's lawyer informed P's lawyer that there would be no sale of the stock. The next day, P's lawyer proposed a payment plan, but D's lawyer rejected anything short of payment in full in cash. P failed to communicate further with D. The next July, D sold the paper for a net of $20,680. P had paid D a total of $29,744.26. P sued to recover the money, and D cross-complained. The trial court found for D and awarded him $34,575, representing the original contract price, less payments P made and the proceeds D received from selling to the third party. P appeals.

Issue. Is it a total breach where a buyer pays about one-third of the purchase price but fails to pay the balance?

Held. Yes. Judgment affirmed.

♦ D was justified in terminating the contract and substituting his legal remedies for his contractual rights only if P's breach was total, rather than partial. If P's breach was partial, D's action would constitute an unlawful repudiation, which would in turn be a total breach that would discharge P from any further duty.

♦ The materiality of a breach determines whether it is partial or complete. Although P had paid part of the purchase price, D was justified in terminating the contract in October because P's offers to perform and his assurances that he would perform were such that it was extremely uncertain whether P actually intended to complete the contract.

♦ Even if D was not justified in treating P's breach as total as of October 5, P's claim that he was discharged as of that date fails. D was not required to perform his promise on that date because P had not tendered the balance due. At best, D's repudiation was anticipatory in nature. But P subsequently disregarded D's repudiation by attempting to arrange an alternative payment plan. D's lawyer told P's lawyer that D would still accept a cash payment; this retraction constitutes a nullification of the original effectiveness of the repudiation.

C. ANTICIPATORY REPUDIATION

1. **Introduction.** Anticipatory repudiation may be treated as a material breach of the contract even before the time for performance. A repudiation consists of words or conduct by one party that a reasonable person would interpret as a refusal to render any further performance. A repudiation excuses the other party from its duty to perform. The rationale is that the innocent party should not be required to wait until the time of performance to seek a remedy if it is clear that the other party will not perform.

   a. **Unconditional refusal.** To constitute an anticipatory repudiation, the act or words must communicate an unconditional refusal to perform as promised. An act that would otherwise be deemed only a minor breach will be treated as a material breach if accompanied by a repudiation.

   b. **Prospective inability to perform.** If one party does not repudiate the contract, but circumstances suggest that that party will not be able to perform as promised, the other party's duty to perform is excused or suspended until the other party performs or provides adequate assurance of performance. [*See* U.C.C. §2-609; Restatement (Second) §251]

2. **Request to Change Contract Term--**

Truman L. Flatt & Sons Co. v. Schupf, 649 N.E.2d 990 (Ill. Ct. App.), *cert. denied*, 657 N.E.2d 640 (Ill. 1995).

Facts. In March, Truman L. Flatt & Sons Co. (P) entered a contract to purchase a parcel of land from Schupf (D). The contract price was $160,000. The contract required a closing on or before June 30, and specified that it was contingent on P obtaining a zoning variance to permit P to build and operate an asphalt plant. On May 21, after a public hearing, P concluded that it could not get the rezoning it required. P offered D $142,500 for the property, reflecting its reduced value under the existing zoning class. D declined the offer. P then informed D that it would proceed with the original purchase price. D notified P that D deemed the contract voided by the new offer to buy for less than the contract price. D arranged to return P's earnest money. P sued for specific performance. The trial court granted D's motion for summary judgment. P appeals.

Issue. Does a request to change a term in a contract amount to anticipatory repudiation of the contract?

Held. No. Judgment reversed.

♦ Anticipatory repudiation can only arise where there is a clear manifestation of an intent not to perform the contract on the date of performance. The intent must be definite and unequivocal; doubtful and indefinite statements are not enough.

♦ As a general rule, a request to change a term in a contract does not amount to a repudiation. D claims that the circumstances made P's request for a lower price an implied threat of nonperformance, but at best, such an inference is weak. The law requires a repudiation to be manifested clearly and unequivocally. The trial court erred in finding P's May 21 letter to be an anticipatory repudiation.

♦ Even if P had repudiated the contract, P timely retracted its repudiation. A statement of repudiation can be nullified by retraction if notification of the retraction comes to the attention of the injured party before he indicates to the other party that he considers the retraction to be final or has materially changed his position in reliance on the repudiation.

♦ If the May 21 letter was an anticipatory breach, D had the right to treat the contract as rescinded or terminated. However, D did not provide P notice or other manifestation of an intent to so treat the contract. Without such notice, P was free to retract its repudiation, so long as D did not materially change its position as a result of the repudiation. Here, D offered no evidence that it changed its position or notified P that it elected to treat the contract as rescinded until after P had retracted its repudiation.

3. Demand for Adequate Assurances--

Hornell Brewing Co. v. Spry, 664 N.Y.S.2d 698 (N.Y. Sup. 1997).

Facts. In 1993, Hornell Brewing Co. (P) orally granted Spry (D) the exclusive right to purchase P's Arizona iced tea products for distribution in Canada. In July 1993, P provided a letter confirming its exclusive distributorship with D but did not explain the details of the agreement. In late 1993, D began being late with its payments to P, and one of D's checks was returned for insufficient funds. D's sales in Canada were far below D's projections. In April, D arranged a conversation between P and Metro Factors, Inc. P sent Metro a letter stating its intention to allow D an outstanding balance of up to $300,000 as long as D paid invoices within 14 days and remained current in its payment obligations. At the time, D had nearly $80,000 in arrearages. Metro wired D the full amount of arrearages on May 9. The same day, D ordered $390,000 to $450,000 worth of products from P. P told D that it would extend D up to $300,000 of credit, based upon D's prior representation that he had secured a $1.5 million line of credit. P also requested that D provide evidence of that line of credit as well as a personal guarantee supported by a verifiable personal financial statement. D never complied with these requirements. Later in May 1994, P de facto terminated its relationship with D and ceased selling its products to D. P sought a declaratory judgment that D's right to distribute P's beverages in Canada has been terminated.

Issue. Is a seller entitled to demand adequate assurance of performance whenever circumstances change so as to show reasonable grounds of insecurity?

Held. Yes. Judgment for P.

♦ The parties had a contract based on the uncontested facts of their conduct. Article 2 of the U.C.C. allows contracts to be formed through conduct. After their oral agreement was reached, D formed a Canadian company, obtained regulatory approvals, and began ordering and distributing P's products, for which D paid, although not on time or in full.

♦ Despite the disputes over the duration and termination of the agreement, P has shown reasonable grounds for insecurity based on D's conduct. As specified by U.C.C. section 2-609(1), P demanded adequate assurance of due performance, and P was justified to suspend performance until it received assurance from D.

♦ Reasonable grounds for insecurity can arise solely from a buyer falling behind in its account with the seller. D claims that once he became current on his account with P, P had no right to demand further assurance. When D became current, his placement of a single order worth $390,000 to $450,000 gave P no chance to learn whether D would meet the 14-day payment terms.

♦ In addition, D had misled P about the scope of his operation, which entitled P to seek further adequate assurance. D's failure to provide such assurance justified P's termination of the agreement.

XI. EXPECTATION DAMAGES: PRINCIPLES AND LIMITATIONS

A. COMPUTING THE VALUE OF PLAINTIFF'S EXPECTATION

1. **Introduction.** Every breach of contract entitles the aggrieved party to sue for damages. The general theory of damages in contract actions is that the injured party should be placed in the same position as if the contract had been properly performed, at least insofar as money can do this; *i.e.*, that the plaintiff should be compensated in money for the loss of her bargain. Compensatory damages, therefore, are designed to give the plaintiff the benefit of the bargain or her reasonable expectation. Compensatory damages consist of two separate and distinct elements:

   a. **The standard measure.** First, a legal formula is applied that measures the loss according to the type of contract involved, which party breached, etc.

   b. **The individualized measure.** In addition to the standard measure, the plaintiff may be entitled to recover those damages that were a consequence of the breach in the particular case at hand. These are called "consequential" damages.

2. **Breach of Real Estate Purchase Contract--**

Roesch v. Bray, 545 N.E.2d 1301 (Ohio Ct. App. 1988).

Facts. The Roeschs (Ps) contracted to sell their home to the Brays (Ds) for $65,000, with $45,000 to be paid at the time of the closing and $20,000 to be paid when Ds sold their home, with no interest to be paid to Ps. Five days later, Ds told Ps they could not perform on the contract. In the meantime, Ps bought another property, borrowing $65,000 at 16% interest. Ps resold the original home a year later for $63,500. Ps sued for breach of contract and recovered $9,163 for utilities, insurance, real estate taxes, maintenance, advertising, and interest on the $45,000 Ds were to have paid at closing. Ps appeal, seeking the difference between the contract price and the later resale price. Ds appeal, claiming that they should not be liable for Ps' costs of holding the property for resale and for the interest on the $45,000.

Issues.

(i) When a buyer defaults on a contract for the sale of real estate, may the seller recover the difference between contract price and the market value of the property at the time of breach?

(ii)   When a buyer breaches a contract to purchase real estate, is the seller entitled to recover the expenses incidental to ownership pending the resale of the property?

Held. (i) Yes. (ii) No. Judgment reversed.

♦   Under Ohio law, when a buyer defaults on a contract for the sale of real estate, the seller can recover the difference between the contract price and the market value of the property at the time of the breach. The trial court in this case did not award this measure because Ps offered no evidence of the market value of the home at the time of breach. The court found that the sale price a year later, on different terms, should not be admitted as evidence.

♦   However, the housing market at the time of the breach was slow because of the high interest rates. The sale a year later was a valid indicator of the market value of the home at the time of breach. The court should have awarded Ps the $1,500 difference between the contract price and the ultimate sale price.

♦   Ds claim that the trial court should not have awarded Ps the costs of holding the property or the interest on the $45,000. Damages for breach of contract are generally limited to losses that are to be reasonably expected as a probable result of the breach. Allowing recovery of utility expenses and maintenance and resale costs could lead to harsh consequences. The duration and extent of such expenses could only be speculated upon, leaving Ds potentially liable for expenses for years on end. Therefore, the court should not have awarded these elements of damage.

Comment. Some jurisdictions would allow recovery of foreseeable expenses such as those this court denied, including maintenance and interest.

---

3.   **Breach of Employment Contract--**

Handicapped Children's Education Board v. Lukaszewski, 332 N.W.2d 774 (Wis. 1983).

Facts. The Handicapped Children's Education Board (P) hired Lukaszewski (D) to work as a speech and language therapist. At the end of the first term, D accepted P's offer to teach for the following school year. In August, prior to the start of the new school year, D took another job closer to her home that also paid more. D notified P that she was resigning. P refused to accept D's resignation and wrote to D's new employer, threatening legal action if D worked for them. D returned to P and began teaching. Soon after, she had a discussion with P's director of special education that left D upset. D's doctor determined that D was experiencing hypertension that would not improve unless the situation changed. He also said it was dangerous for D to drive the long distance to P's location. Based on this doctor's statement, D resigned again and returned to the other employer. P hired a replacement for D, but had to pay $1,026.64 more for salary. P sued D, claiming as damages the $1,026.64 in extra salary. The court found for P. The court of appeals affirmed as to D's breach, but reversed as to the award for the higher salary on the basis that P obtained a more valuable teacher. The Wisconsin Supreme Court granted P's petition for review.

Issue. If an employee breaches her employment contract by quitting, may the employer recover damages for the extra salary it has to pay to a replacement?

Held. Yes. Judgment reversed in part.

♦ The trial court found that D quit her job with P for reasons other than her health. As D's resignation was not justified, D breached the contract.

♦ An employer may recover damages from an employee who fails to perform an employment contract. Damages are measured by the parties' expectations, and in an employment contract case, damages can include the cost of obtaining other services equivalent to that promised but not performed.

♦ It was within the contemplation of the parties that P would have to hire a replacement. The higher salary for the replacement was based on a salary schedule established between the teachers' union and P; this suggests that the replacement was a more valuable teacher. The court of appeals incorrectly focused on the value of the services instead of on the expectations of the parties. P did not want or need a more experienced teacher. P mitigated its damages by hiring the least expensive, qualified replacement available. P is entitled to have the benefit of its bargain restored.

Dissent. D's resignation was justified by the undisputed medical evidence. It does not matter whether D's medical condition may have been self-induced, as the trial court found.

Comment. As a general rule, a court will not order an employee to specifically perform.

---

4. Breach of Construction Contract--

American Standard, Inc. v. Schectman, 439 N.Y.S.2d 529 (N.Y. App. Div.), *appeal denied*, 427 N.E.2d 512 (N.Y. 1981).

Facts. American Standard, Inc. (P) decided to close its pig iron manufacturing plant. P sold all of its buildings and equipment to Schectman (D) for $275,000 in return for D's promise to remove the equipment, demolish the structures, and grade the property as specified. D failed to remove all the foundations and other structures below the grade line. P sued. The trial court rejected D's defense that his breach did not affect the value of the property, since P sold it for $183,000, which was only $3,000 less than its full fair market value. Instead, the trial court instructed the jury that the proper measure of damages was the cost of completion, which P's expert estimated at $110,500. The jury awarded P $90,000 in damages. D appeals.

Issue. Where a party has substantially performed, but the cost to complete is still $90,000, may the other party recover the completion cost even when the fair market value of the property is essentially unaffected by the incomplete work?

Held. Yes. Judgment affirmed.

♦ The general rule of damages for breach of a construction contract allows recovery for any damages that are the direct, natural, and immediate consequence of the breach and that were within the contemplation of the parties when the contract was made. Where the contractor's performance was defective or incomplete, the reasonable cost of replacement or completion is the measure.

♦ When the contractor has substantially performed, however, and the correction of defects would result in economic waste, the proper measure is the difference between the value of the property as constructed and the value if performance had been properly completed. However, the cases demonstrate that the type of economic waste that justifies the diminution in value rule occurs in situations where defects are irremediable or cannot be repaired without substantially tearing down the structure.

♦ If the contractor breaches a covenant that is merely incidental to the main purpose of the contract and completion would be disproportionately costly, courts have applied the diminution in value measure. Courts also consider whether the contractor showed substantial performance made in good faith and did not breach intentionally.

♦ In this case, the grading and removal of structures were central to the contract. The cost of completion measure would be the ordinary measure for D's breach, and would be within the contemplation of the parties when the contract was made. That completion would have added little or nothing to the value of the property does not excuse the default. A landowner is free to build structures on his property that even reduce the value of the property.

♦ To complete the work in this case would not require undoing anything that was done in good faith; it is merely work that D left undone. The cost of completion suggests that D had not rendered substantial performance or that the work left undone was of trivial importance. Besides, D's breach was intentional, as he interpreted the contract not to require the work, despite the contract's plain language.

B. FORESEEABILITY, CERTAINTY, AND CAUSATION

1. **Foreseeability.** In addition to the standard measure of damages, the breaching party is liable for all losses resulting from his breach that the parties as reasonable persons should have foreseen as likely to result from the breach at the time the contract was made.

    a. **General rule.** The standard measure does not provide full compensation for the loss of the benefit of the bargain when there are special circumstances that may aggravate the economic loss to one party if the other fails to perform. If such special circumstances were known to both parties at the time the contract was made, the breaching party will be deemed to have assumed the liability for such additional damages in the event of breach. [*See* U.C.C. §2-715(2); Restatement (Second) §351]

    b. **Early case--**

Hadley v. Baxendale, 156 Eng. Rep. 145 (1854).

Facts. The Hadleys (Ps) stopped operation of their mill when a crank shaft broke. They contracted with Baxendale (D) to have it shipped to the manufacturer for repairs. D's employees were negligent in not completing delivery within a reasonable time, and for five days Ps lost profits and wages paid. D had not been informed that the mill would not operate until the shaft was repaired. The jury awarded Ps damages. D appeals.

Issue. May the nonbreaching party recover damages for losses it sustains but which would not ordinarily be expected?

Held. No. New trial ordered.

◆   Normally, damages are those that arise naturally from a breach of the contract (*i.e.,* those that would be expected by both parties to probably flow from a breach).

◆   In addition, where there are damages because of special circumstances (here, lost profits due to the mill shutdown), they will be assessed against the defendant only where they were reasonably within the contemplation of both parties as being the probable consequence of a breach. Here, D did not know that the mill was shut down and would be until the new shaft arrived.

◆   Since lost profits would not ordinarily flow from D's breach, and since the special circumstances were never communicated to D, loss of profits should not have been considered in estimating damages.

◆   Case remanded for a new trial to determine the proper award of damages.

---

c. **Awareness of "special circumstances."** Since the doctrine rests on the assumption that the breaching party was aware at the time he contracted of the losses likely to result in the event of his breach, it must always be shown that he had (or as a reasonable person should have had) a clear understanding of the "special circumstances" facing the other party. A generalized knowledge of the other's business affairs is not enough. Note that in the complex modern business world it may usually be impractical to give the other party sufficient notice of special circumstances. For example, delay of an executive's flight might cause him to miss an important meeting, but the airline cannot respond to all such special circumstances.

2. **Certainty.** An additional limitation on the plaintiff's right to recover damages is that the amount of his loss must be reasonably certain of computation. Damages that are uncertain (*i.e.,* "speculative") are not allowed because any award exceeding the plaintiff's actual losses would in effect be a penalty, and punitive damages are not allowed in contract actions. If the amount of the plaintiff's damages cannot be made certain, the plaintiff can recover no more than nominal damages for the defendant's breach. This limitation is encountered most frequently where the measure of damages relates to the "profits" of some business or venture.

3. **Lost Profits from a Collateral Contract--**

Florafax International, Inc. v. GTE Market Resources, Inc., 933 P.2d 282 (Okla. 1997).

Facts. Florafax International, Inc. (P) acted as a clearinghouse for florists around the United States and internationally. One of P's clients was Bellerose Floral, Inc., a leading marketer of floral products that handled between 100,000 and 200,000 orders annually. Bellerose contracted with P so that P would handle calls on Bellerose's 1-800-FLOWERS phone number. Two weeks later, P contracted with GTE Market Resources, Inc. (D) to have D provide telecommunications and telemarketing services for P. The contract had a three-year term, but was terminable after two years. The contract specified that, in the event D breached, D would pay P consequential damages and lost profits. D knew that Bellerose was P's largest customer. D knew that it would make little or no money on its contract with P and began having problems handling P's business because D did not hire enough people. Eventually, D's failure to perform caused Bellerose to terminate its agreement with P. P sued D for the profits it lost on its contract with Bellerose, claiming that Bellerose would have increased its sales volume 100%, amounting to a loss of over $1.9 million. D's expert claimed that the growth would have been much less, for a total loss of around $500,000. The jury awarded P $750,000 for the lost Bellerose account, plus $820,000 in costs to set up a call center to replace D. D appeals.

Issue. May damages for breach of contract include profits from third-party collateral contracts?

Held. Yes. Judgment affirmed.

♦ Loss of future or anticipated profit is recoverable in a breach of contract action if the loss is: (i) within the contemplation of the parties when the contract was made; (ii) flows directly or proximately from the breach; and (iii) is capable of reasonably accurate measurement or estimate.

♦ In this case, there was sufficient evidence that D knew about the Bellerose account. The contract itself referred to lost profits as a measure of damages. The loss of profits on the Bellerose contract was thus within the contemplation of the parties.

♦ D claims that because P's contract with Bellerose included a 60-day cancellation clause, P's recovery should be limited to 60 days' worth of lost profits. However, P's contract with D had a minimum two-year period. D cannot benefit from a cancellation right it had no ability to exercise.

♦ P cannot recover damages based on mere speculation or conjecture, but uncertainty as to the exact amount of damages does not prevent recovery. There was evidence about the lost profits that supports the jury's finding. Bellerose had been in business for many years and had a demonstrable track record. The jury award was within the range provided by the expert witnesses.

C. MITIGATION OF DAMAGES

1. **Introduction.** A party seeking a remedy for breach of contract has a duty to use reasonable efforts to mitigate damages. Under U.C.C. section 2-715(2), when a seller breaches, the buyer has a right to cover by obtaining substitute goods; if the buyer fails to cover, it cannot recover consequential damages it would have avoided by covering.

2. **Continuation of Performance After Notice of Breach--**

Rockingham County v. Luten Bridge Co., 35 F.2d 301 (4th Cir. 1929).

Facts. Luten Bridge Co. (P) contracted to build a bridge for Rockingham County (D). D changed its mind and gave notice of cancellation to P before actual construction began. P went ahead and built the bridge anyway, even though there was no road leading to it. P sued to recover the contract price and won. D appeals.

Issue. May a party continue performance after notice of breach and recover the full contract amount?

Held. No. Judgment reversed.

- ♦ D clearly breached the contract without a right to do so, but once P had received notice of the breach, it had a duty not to increase its damages.

- ♦ A plaintiff's remedy is to treat the contract as broken when it receives notice and seek damages, including expected profits as well as any losses it suffered. Thus, P may recover its lost profits and expenses incurred prior to notice of the breach.

Comments.

- ♦ Compare the remedy available to sellers of manufactured goods in U.C.C. section 2-704(2).

- ♦ The nonbreaching party need not choose the least expensive substitute performance, so long as the choice made is reasonable under the circumstances.

---

3. **Mitigation in Employment Contracts.**

    a. **Employer's breach.** When the employer breaches, the employee generally is entitled to recover the full contract price (wages not yet paid at the time of the breach), subject to her duty to mitigate damages.

    b. **Employee's breach.** When the employee breaches, the employer may recover whatever it costs to replace the employee. However, the employee's death or illness discharges her obligation under the doctrine of "impossibility of performance."

    c. **Mitigation.** If the employer wrongfully terminates the employment, the employee has an affirmative duty to use reasonable efforts to locate similar work. The employer has the burden to show that such work was available. The more specialized the employee, the more difficult it may be for the employer to show that comparable work was available. Also, the employee has a duty not to increase her damages by continuing performance after the employer's breach.

    d. **Lower paying job in mitigation--**

Havill v. Woodstock Soapstone Company, Inc., 865 A.2d 335 (Vt. 2004).

Facts. Lois Havill (P) worked intermittently for Woodstock Soapstone Company, Inc. (D) for approximately 15 years, for a total of over 10 years' actual employment. Although she worked part time during part of this period, she worked full time for the last three and one-half years of her employment. D issued personnel policies that provided that an employee was entitled to two written warnings in a 12-month period before termination. P had positive performance reviews. Because business was declining, D reorganized the company and hired Laura Scott to streamline the operation. P and Scott had conflicts. P received a letter of reprimand, which was not considered a warning, from D's president. P agreed to cooperate with Scott, but a little over a month later, D terminated her without providing any written warnings or other explanation. D provided P with a recommendation letter to help her find a new job. Two weeks later, D advertised for office help, and within a few months hired three new employees, all of whom performed some of the functions that P had done. P sued. The court found that D had terminated P without following its own procedures, thereby breaching its employment contract. The court awarded P $74,644 in damages plus $15,040 in prejudgment interest. This represented seven years of damages for lost wages—five years of back pay and two years of front pay. P found temporary work at a reduced salary only three days after D terminated her. After the temporary employment of almost three years, she became self-employed. D appeals the damages award.

Issue. Where an employer improperly terminates an employee, may the employer be required to compensate the employee for future lost wages through retirement age where the employee obtains substitute employment at a lower salary?

Held. Yes. Judgment affirmed as to liability, affirmed in part and reversed in part as to damages, and case remanded for reconsideration of damages award.

- ♦ The length of employment before termination is a factor in determining whether a front pay damage award is reasonable and not too speculative. D argues that the three and one-half year period when P was a full-time employee should determine the damages period. But the employment relationship began almost 15 years before the date of termination and comprised a total of over 10 years of P's actual employment. This supports the damages period determined by the trial court.

- ♦ However, we remand this issue for other reasons. The trial court found that P, who was 58 when D terminated her, intended to work until age 70 but that her post-trial memorandum suggested that the award be based on the normal retirement age of 65. The trial court misunderstood her request, but the court is not required to grant P's request as long as the award is limited to a reasonable time that is not too speculative. Also, P had performance-related issues that could have eventually led to her termination at an earlier point.

- ♦ D claims that the court erred in finding that P had fully mitigated damages. However, P did obtain another job, even if the pay was lower. D did not carry its burden of showing that P could have found a better job.

- ♦ D points out that for several years while P was employed with D and later during her temporary employment, P worked from home for Therapeutic Dimensions to supplement her income. She was then working a total of 55 to 60 hours per week. After becoming self-employed, she has continued to work for Therapeutic, and also for Quest, for a total of 40 hours per week. Therapeutic has become one of P's two primary sources of income. This change in character must be reflected in the calculation of damages. D argues that it should not be responsible for compensating P for what appears to be a voluntary choice to work fewer total hours now than she did when she worked for D. The trial court excluded the Therapeutic income from the damages determination and thus unfairly placed the burden on D to make up for the decrease in P's income that resulted more from her choice to work fewer hours than D's decision to terminate her. The trial court should treat income from Therapeutic the same way it treats income from Quest for the period after her termination from her temporary job.

♦ The trial court may have erred in granting P damages for vacation time that her subsequent jobs did not give her, because the court did not consider P's past behavior regarding vacation time. On remand, the court should consider whether P would have taken vacation time and therefore not worked as many hours, since her base pay included paid vacations.

♦ Although D was not contractually bound to pay P bonuses, the court's decision to include a reasonably anticipated bonus was not speculative, because P regularly received such bonuses. However, the court erred in granting P annual pay raises, because P did not receive raises every year.

---

4. Mitigation and the Lost Volume Seller--

Jetz Service Co. v. Salina Properties, 865 P.2d 1051 (Kan. Ct. App. 1993).

Facts. Jetz Service Co. (P) supplied and maintained coin-operated laundry equipment in 2,000 locations. P entered a six-year lease with the predecessor in title to Salina Properties (D). P paid $3,000 in a decorating allowance and was entitled to the first $300 per month, or 50 percent, of the gross receipts, whichever was greater. Sixteen months before the lease term expired, D replaced P's laundry equipment with its own. P eventually placed the equipment into another of its locations, but P sued for lost profits. D claimed that P had not mitigated its damages, but the trial court found that P was a "lost volume" lessee and awarded P $6,383 in lost profits and $2,165 in attorney's fees. D appeals.

Issue. May a lost volume seller recover damages for lost profits even if he sells the goods to a third party?

Held. Yes. Judgment affirmed.

♦ P clearly was entitled to lost profits for the period until it placed the laundry equipment in another location. From that point on, P would have to reduce its damages by the amount it earned from the equipment in the other location, unless P was a lost volume lessee.

♦ A lost volume seller is one who, even though he sells the property to a third party, still lost money on the original sale contract that the buyer breached. It applies where a seller has a large enough supply of products that he could have completed both sales had the buyer not breached. A lost volume seller is entitled to damages reflecting the volume of business lost due to the breach.

♦ D claims that the lost volume theory should only apply to a seller of goods under U.C.C. section 2-708(2), not to a provider of services. However, the concept applies as well to a volume provider of services as it does to a volume seller of goods. P had several warehouses containing laundry equipment that it could install in leased locations. P could have provided other equipment to the new location while leaving the original equipment at D's facility.

D. NONRECOVERABLE DAMAGES

1. **Introduction.** For reasons of public policy, a party injured by breach of contract may not recover for every conceivable injury. The law of contracts reflects practical commercial realities, and one of the essential factors that people consider in entering a contract is the associated risk. Limiting contract remedies to those that are foreseeable and can be quantified allows people to make reasoned choices among various risk potentials.

2. **American Rule on Attorneys' Fees--**

Zapata Hermanos Sucesores, S.A. v. Hearthside Baking Co., 2001 WL 1000927 (N.D. Ill. 2001).

Facts. Zapata Hermanos Sucesores, S.A. (P), was a Mexican manufacturer of tin cans. P sold tin cans to Hearthside Baking Co. (D), a United States corporation. When D had accumulated a debt of $800,000, P refused to deliver any more cans until D became current with its payments. D told P that if P refused to ship cans, D would never pay P. P sued D in Illinois to recover the debt. D denied liability, which forced P to incur substantial expenses for litigation. P prevailed at trial and sought to recover its attorneys' fees. The parties' contract was governed by a treaty entitled, "The Convention on the International Sale of Goods." The Convention provided that damages for breach of contract were limited to those that the party in breach foresaw or ought to have foreseen when the parties entered the contract, but did not specify litigation expenses.

Issue. May the prevailing party recover its attorneys' fees when the losing party denied liability in bad faith?

Held. Yes. Judgment for P.

♦ The treaty that governs this case requires uniformity of construction. The courts cannot impose the American Rule on attorneys' fees, even though P sued D in an American court.

♦ Litigation expenses, including attorneys' fees, were foreseeable costs in the event litigation became necessary. P incurred these expenses as a consequence of D's breach; hence, attorneys' fees are consequential damages under the Convention.

♦ Apart from the Convention, American courts have the inherent power to impose a litigant's fees on its adversary where the adversary has acted in bad faith or for oppressive reasons. D here acted in bad faith when it threatened not to pay P unless P continued shipping, despite D's large past due balance. D further made it as expensive and difficult as possible for P to recover in this litigation by answering the complaint with a general denial despite having no defense to P's claims.

Comment. Sales of goods between American companies are governed by the U.C.C., which does not allow attorneys' fees as incidental or consequential damages.

---

3. Emotional Distress Not a Contract Remedy--

Erlich v. Menezes, 981 P.2d 978 (Cal. 1999).

Facts. The Erlichs (Ps) contracted to have their "dreamhouse" built on their ocean-view lot by Menezes (D). Two months after they moved in, a rain storm caused extensive leaks throughout the house, leaving three inches of standing water in the living room and ceilings collapsing. D was unable to fix the leaks. Another engineer found extensive structural problems with the house, including roof beams and decks that were in danger of collapsing. Ps sued for damages, including emotional distress that aggravated a heart condition. The jury awarded Ps $406,700 for the cost of repairs, plus $50,000 to each spouse for emotional distress and $50,000 to the husband for physical pain and suffering. The court of appeals affirmed. D appeals.

Issue. May homeowners recover damages for emotional distress based upon breach of a contract to build a house?

Held. No. Judgment reversed.

♦ Contract damages are limited to those within the contemplation of the parties when they entered the contract; unforeseeable damages are not recoverable. This approach encourages commercial activity by allowing parties to estimate the financial risks of their business dealings. In contrast, tort damages are awarded as full compensation for all injury suffered, whether it was anticipated or not. Tort damages have uncertain boundaries that would undermine commercial activity if they were applied to contract law.

♦ A contract may create a legal duty, the violation of which may support an action in tort; however, conduct constituting a breach of contract becomes tortious only when it also violates a duty independent of the contract arising from principles of tort law.

♦ Tort damages could arise in a contract case where a breach of duty directly causes physical injury, where a contract was fraudulently induced, or where the contract involved insurance, where there is a special fiduciary responsibility between insurer and insured. Mere foreseeability of an injury does not create a duty, however.

♦ The mere negligent breach of a contract is not sufficient to create tort liability. In this case, there was no special relationship between Ps and D that could give rise to tort liability. The jury found that D did not act intentionally and that he was not guilty of fraud or misrepresentation.

♦ Building a home may be a stress-free project, but it is more commonly a stressful project with a high likelihood of errors being made. Ps' emotional suffering derived from an inherently economic concern.

♦ Damages for emotional distress are generally not recoverable in an action for breach of ordinary commercial contracts. Cases that do allow such recovery typically involve mental anguish arising from more personal undertakings, such as misdiagnosed disease, a child injured during childbirth, etc. These cases involve contracts in which emotional concerns are the essence of the contract. Adding a risk of damages for emotional distress to commercial agreements would make the financial risks difficult to predict.

♦ Expanding liability for breach of construction contracts is a task for the legislature, which is suited to considering the broad economic consequences of such a rule.

E. BUYERS' AND SELLERS' REMEDIES UNDER THE UNIFORM COMMERCIAL CODE

1. **Introduction.** The standard measure of damages for breach of contract for the sale of goods is the difference between the contract price and the market price for the goods at the time and place where the goods were to be delivered. This is true whether the breach was committed by the seller or by the buyer. [U.C.C. §§2-708, 2-713]

2. **Buyers' Remedies—Cancellation.** U.C.C. section 2-711(1) allows a buyer to cancel the contract if: (i) the seller fails to deliver the goods; (ii) the seller repudiates the contract; (iii) the buyer properly rejects the goods; or (iv) the buyer revokes acceptance. The key is whether the buyer is justified in rejecting the goods or revoking acceptance because the goods do not conform to the contract.

3. **Buyers' Remedies—Damages.** The appropriate measure of a buyer's damages depends on the facts of the case.

    a. **Cover.** Under U.C.C. section 2-712, a buyer may "cover," or purchase substitute goods, and recover the difference between the cover price and the contract price. The substitute goods must be commercially reasonable substitutes.

    b. **Market damages.** The buyer may claim the standard measure of damages, which is the difference between the market price at the time the buyer learned of the breach and the contract price, less expenses saved due to the seller's breach. [U.C.C. §2-713]

    c. **Damages for nonconforming goods.** Under U.C.C. section 2-714(1), the buyer may accept nonconforming goods and then seek damages caused by the seller's breach in the ordinary course of events. This can include cost of repair and difference in value.

    d. **Incidental and consequential damages.** The buyer may recover incidental and consequential damages arising from the seller's breach, subject to the ordinary limitations associated with these measures of damage. Foreseeability limits consequential damages that are economic, but personal or property injuries resulting from breach of warranty need not be foreseeable. [U.C.C. §2-715]

4. **Specific Performance.** U.C.C. section 2-716 codifies the general rule on specific performance.

5. **Sellers' Remedies.** A seller has a right to recover for a buyer's refusal to purchase under a contract for the sale of goods.

    a. **Right to resell.** Upon a buyer's refusal to purchase the goods contracted for, the seller has the right to sell the goods in a commercially reasonable manner. If she does so, she can recover from the buyer the difference between the contract price and the resale price, rather than merely the difference between the contract price and the market price. [U.C.C. §2-706]

        1) Under U.C.C. section 2-708, a seller who does not resell is limited to the "contract price-market price" differential.

2) If the seller does resell the goods, she is not accountable to the buyer for any profit made on the resale. [U.C.C. §2-708]

b. **Action for full price—seller unable to resell "identified goods."** Where the buyer has breached by refusing to purchase goods which have already been "identified" to the contract, and the seller is unable to resell the goods after reasonable efforts (or such efforts would be unavailing), the seller may recover the full contract price. [U.C.C. §2-709]

F. JUSTIFICATIONS FOR EXPECTATION DAMAGE RULE

1. **Economic Analysis of Contract Law.** There are several rationales for allowing a party to recover expectation damages for a wholly executory contract, even where the party has done nothing more than sign the contract. One of these is the notion that the execution of a contract creates a property right, the deprivation or destruction of which should be actionable. Another aspect of economic analysis is the concept of "efficient breach," whereby a party would breach its contract simply if it were more profitable to breach than to perform. In this sense, contract damages are not designed to prevent breach but only to compensate the injured party. Another approach favors punishing breach by forcing the breaching party to transfer its gain to the nonbreaching party. The courts may not expressly state that this is what they are doing, but application of the law can have this effect.

2. **Damages Based on Breaching Party's Gain--**

Roth v. Speck, 126 A.2d 153 (D.C. 1956).

Facts. Roth (P) owned a beauty salon. He hired Speck (D) to work for him as a hairdresser for one year at a salary of $75 per week or 50 percent of the gross receipts from his work, whichever was greater. D worked for about six and one-half months before quitting. To replace D, P hired another person to whom he paid $350 before letting him go. He hired a second replacement, but was losing money on his work. In the meantime, D was earning $100 per week at his new employer. P sued for breach of contract. The trial court awarded P nominal damages of $1. P appeals.

Issue. Where an employee breaches an employment contract, is the employer entitled to recover the cost of obtaining replacement services as measured by the former employee's higher salary at his new employer?

Held. Yes. Judgment reversed.

♦ The measure of damages when an employee breaches an employment contract is the cost of obtaining another service equivalent to that promised and not performed.

- To replace D, P would have had to pay $100 per week to get a hairdresser as talented as D. P should be entitled to recover the difference between D's original salary of $75 and his value of $100, multiplied by the remaining 24 weeks in the contract.

Comment. D failed to offer evidence that his actual salary was greater than $75 because of the profit-sharing arrangement.

———————

XII. ALTERNATIVES TO EXPECTATION DAMAGES: RELIANCE AND RESTITUTIONARY DAMAGES, SPECIFIC PERFORMANCE, AND AGREED REMEDIES

A. RELIANCE DAMAGES

1. **Introduction.** The reliance measure of damages focuses on the nonbreaching party's costs. This measure aims at putting the nonbreaching party in the position it would have been in had the promise not been made in the first place. It is used when the promise is enforceable only because it was relied upon.

2. **Development Costs--**

Wartzman v. Hightower Productions, Ltd., 456 A.2d 82 (Md. Ct. Spec. App. 1983).

Facts. Hightower Productions, Ltd. (P) was formed to employ an entertainer named Woody Hightower, who would live in a flagpole perch for several months as a publicity stunt. P's principals consulted Wartzman (D), a lawyer, to help them with incorporating. P sold $43,000 worth of stock to generate capital to build the perch, create publicity, and otherwise develop the project. P ran low on funds and scheduled another shareholders' meeting to raise more, but D informed it that it could not sell any more stock because the company had been structured wrong. D had failed to prepare an offering memorandum as required by state law. It would cost up to $15,000 to hire a specialist to prepare this document. When it turned out that Woody could not be exhibited across state lines because of the stock problem, the shareholders abandoned the project. P sued D, claiming damages for individual and corporate indebtedness incurred in reliance on D's work, as well as accrued expenses. The jury awarded P $170,508.43. D appeals.

Issue. May a party recover its development costs incurred in reliance on the breaching party's proper performance of its duties?

Held. Yes. Judgment affirmed.

- D claims there was an insufficient nexus between his failure to properly advise P and P's failure as a business; otherwise, D would be in the position of an insurer of P's success. However, P's need to raise adequate capital was the main reason P hired D. P's inability to raise capital was the direct cause of the project's collapse. No greater nexus is required.

- A contracting party is only liable for damages arising from risks that were foreseeable at the time the contract was made. A client who hires an attorney such as D has a right to D's diligence, knowledge, and skill. D is properly held liable for the loss that P incurred as a result of D's failure to properly advise P.

- D sought a jury instruction that P should not recover if P would not have been able to raise the money regardless of D's breach. However, P's claim was based on reliance damages, not lost profits. There was no basis for asking the jury to speculate on the ultimate success of P's venture.

- D claims that P could have mitigated its damages by hiring the specialist, but a party who is in default may not mitigate damages by showing that the other party could have reduced the damages by spending even more money. The doctrine of avoidable consequences does not apply when both parties have an equal opportunity to mitigate damages. D could have hired the securities expert, but declined to do so.

---

3. Reliance Limited to Out-of-Pocket Expenses--

Walser v. Toyota Motor Sales, U.S.A., Inc., 43 F.3d 396 (8th Cir. 1994).

Facts. Walser and his partner (Ps) owned a BMW dealership and a Lincoln-Mercury dealership. They met with Haag, a representative of Toyota Motor Sales, U.S.A., Inc. (D) to see about getting a Lexus dealership. Ps formally applied for the dealership. Haag later told Ps that a letter of intent had been approved for them. A few days later, Haag called them back to say that a mistake had been made and that D needed additional financial information. In the meantime, Walser's father had contracted to purchase property for the Lexus dealership. Eventually, D decided not to give Ps the dealership. Ps sued on breach of contract and other theories. The jury awarded Ps $232,131 in out-of-pocket expenses based on promissory estoppel. Ps appeal.

Issue. Is a claim for damages under promissory estoppel limited to out-of-pocket expenses?

Held. Yes. Judgment affirmed.

- Ps claim that they were entitled to recover lost profits of up to $7.6 million. To the extent that the jury relied on promissory estoppel, however, damages may be measured by the extent of Ps' reliance rather than by the terms of the promise.

- The limitation of damages to out-of-pocket expenses is allowed, but not required, by state law, as explained in section 90 of the Restatement (Second) of Contracts. In this case, the court did not abuse its discretion in so limiting Ps' damages. The dealership was far from a certainty and D showed that Ps would have a difficult time meeting the capitalization requirements. Haag notified Ps within just a few days that he had been mistaken about the letter of intent. Ps did not lose any opportunity by relying on Haag's statement.

- The court also did not err in limiting Ps' damages to the difference between the actual value of the property and the price paid for it. That reflects the actual damages Ps incurred, since they still owned the property.

B. RESTITUTIONARY DAMAGES

1. **Introduction.** If a breach results in a failure of consideration, such as where the performing party did not render substantial performance, the nonbreaching party may unilaterally rescind the contract and sue for restitution of whatever benefits were conferred upon the breaching party. One often-used term is quasi-contract, which means that although there is no enforceable contract, the defendant has received a benefit, his retention of which is inequitable. This is also called recovery in *quantum meruit.*

   a. **Definition.** A quasi-contract does not involve mutual assent but is a fictitious promise implied by law to avoid unjust enrichment of the defendant at the plaintiff's expense.

   b. **Elements.** To recover in quasi-contract the reasonable value of a benefit conferred, the plaintiff must show:

      1) That he has rendered services or expended property that *confers a benefit* on the defendant;

      2) That he did so with the *expectation of being compensated*;

      3) That he *was not acting as an intermeddler*; and

      4) That unless the defendant compensates the plaintiff, the defendant will be *unjustly enriched* at the plaintiff's expense.

2. Recovery in Restitution Despite Actual Loss If Contract Had Been Performed--

United States v. Algernon Blair, Inc., 479 F.2d 638 (4th Cir. 1973).

Facts. Coastal Steel Erectors, Inc., a subcontractor suing in the name of the United States (P), had contracted with Algernon Blair, Inc. (D) to supply certain equipment and perform steel erection as part of D's construction of a United States naval hospital. P performed about 28% of the subcontract before it terminated its performance, citing D's refusal to pay for crane rental. P sued to recover for labor and equipment furnished. The trial court held that P's termination was justified, but that while P was entitled to $37,000 in restitution, it would have lost a like amount had it completed performance and therefore should receive nothing. P appeals.

Issue. May a plaintiff recover in restitution even if he would have recovered nothing in a suit on the contract?

Held. Yes. Judgment reversed.

- ♦ An accepted principle of contract law is that the promisee upon breach has the option to forgo any suit on the contract and claim only the reasonable value of his performance. This is true even where the complaint joins a quantum meruit claim with a claim for damages from breach of contract.

- ♦ D has retained benefits, conferred at P's own expense, without having fully paid for them. This entitles P to restitution in quantum meruit. Such relief is appropriate regardless of whether P would have lost money on the contract and been unable to recover in a suit on the contract. P should recover the reasonable value of its performance, undiminished by any loss it would have suffered by fully performing.

3. Modern Rule Permitting Recovery by Defaulting Party--

Lancellotti v. Thomas, 491 A.2d 117 (Pa. Super. Ct. 1985).

Facts. Lancellotti (P) agreed to purchase Thomas's (D's) luncheonette business and to rent the premises from D for a five-year term, with an option to renew for an additional five years. One condition to the lease was that P would build an addition to the existing business; in return, P was forgiven the first month's rent. Originally, the lease was to terminate if P failed to build the addition, but later the parties agreed that if P failed, P would owe the rent otherwise deferred. P made the agreed down payment, but the parties began arguing over the addition. P refused to build it, so D did, relying on P's alleged promise to reimburse D. P decided not to continue the business, and D resumed operations. P sued for the refund of its down payment. Applying the common law rule, the trial court held that P, as the breaching party, could not recover the payment. P appeals.

Issue. May a defaulting party recover part of the payment made prior to the default?

Held. Yes. Judgment reversed and case remanded.

♦ Under common law, the majority rule prevented a defaulting party from recovering on the theory that the party who breaches should not obtain an *advantage* from his own wrong. This rule does not take into account the possible windfall the nonbreaching party could obtain, however, and the more the breaching party performed, the greater the windfall.

♦ Because the common law rule effectively constitutes a penalty against the defaulting party, the Restatement permits restitution even for the party in breach to the extent of any benefit conferred in excess of the loss caused by the breach. This does not apply, however, if by the terms of the contract the performance is to be retained as reasonable liquidated damages.

♦ An additional factor that has prompted the modern rejection of the common law rule is that the U.C.C. permits a breaching party to recover restitution.

♦ The modern trend should be adopted in this state because contract law is not intended to punish. On remand, the court should determine whether P is entitled to restitution, and if so, how much is reasonable, if any.

Dissent. There is no authority in this state for the adoption of the Restatement rule; the traditional rule is still in effect here.

---

4.   **Recovery Based on Unjust Enrichment--**

Ventura v. Titan Sports, Inc., 65 F.3d 725 (8th Cir. 1995), *cert. denied*, 516 U.S. 1174 (1996).

Facts. Ventura (P), a professional wrestler, began working for Titan Sports, Inc. (D) in the spring of 1984 under an oral contract. In late 1984, P stopped wrestling and became a commentator for D, again under an oral contract. P received $1,000 per week. The parties did not discuss videotape royalties or licenses, although D was producing videotapes. In 1985, P signed a contract for wrestling services, called a WBA. In 1986, he stopped working for D for a few months before returning to work as a commentator under an oral agreement. In 1987, P's agent, Bloom, agreed to a written contract that waived royalties, based on D's statement to Bloom that D's policy was to pay royalties only to "feature" performers. P worked under this contract until 1990. Starting in 1984, D produced about 90 videotapes that included P. P sued for misrepresentation and quantum meruit. The jury found that D had defrauded P and awarded P $801,333.06 in damages for D's use of P's commentary on the videotapes, and $8,625.60 for D's use of P's name, voice, and likeness in other merchandise. D appeals, claiming that P was not entitled to recovery under quantum meruit.

Issue. May a party recover under quantum meruit when he was fully compensated for his services but the employer benefits from those services in a manner beyond what the contract contemplated?

Held. Yes. Judgment affirmed.

♦ The basic rule on quantum meruit, or unjust enrichment, is that where one party was unjustly enriched based on failure of consideration, fraud, mistake, or other situations where it would be morally wrong for one party to enrich himself at the expense of another, the other may recover.

♦ The only services that P provided to D were those provided pursuant to P's agreements with D. However, those agreements do not address all of the benefit created by P's services. D could be unjustly enriched if it used P's performance in ways beyond the limits of the contracts and without P's consent.

♦ D's right to use P's performance was limited by P's publicity rights. Minnesota would recognize the tort of violation of publicity rights, which protects an individual's pecuniary interests in publicity. P's WBA contract precluded royalties for P's performance as a wrestler, but the parties had no agreement about royalties for D's exploitation of P's performance as a commentator prior to P's agent Bloom becoming involved. Accordingly, D violated P's publicity rights during this period and quantum meruit is an appropriate remedy.

♦ The contracts negotiated by Bloom did address videotape royalties, but D fraudulently induced P to sign these contracts by telling P that D paid royalties only to featured performers. In fact, D was paying royalties to other performers who were not featured performers. P relied on D's false representations. Fraud is a proper basis for recovery under unjust enrichment and quantum meruit.

♦ D challenged P's use of an expert witness regarding the appropriate royalty rate, but the expert used reliable data and made reasonable inferences based on other similar royalty arrangements.

Dissent. There is no right of publicity in Minnesota. No Minnesota court has specifically adopted such a right, and the courts have not adopted the tort of invasion of privacy, which is virtually indistinguishable from a right of publicity. At least with respect to the pre-Bloom videotapes, it would not be inequitable for D to reproduce and sell videotapes of performances for which D paid P. P is simply seeking additional compensation for having performed no additional work, while D already paid P for his services, did all the work involved in producing and distributing the videotapes, and assumed all the business risk. P was employed to "broadcast wrestling" on television. The law resolves ambiguities in this area in favor of the licensee, who should be allowed to pursue any uses that reasonably fall within the medium described in the license.

C. SPECIFIC PERFORMANCE

1. **Introduction.** Specific performance is an equitable remedy whereby a court orders a breaching party to perform. As an equitable remedy, specific performance is available only when available legal remedies are inadequate. One of the traditional justifications for specific performance is that the goods are unique, so no monetary damages will suffice.

2. **Option Contract--**

City Stores Co. v. Ammerman, 266 F. Supp. 766 (D.D.C. 1967), *aff'd,* 394 F.2d 950 (D.C. Cir. 1968).

Facts. To get the necessary zoning for a shopping center, Ammerman (D) offered City Stores Co. (P) a place in the center on a favorable rental basis in return for P's favorable letter to the zoning board. D got the zoning, but refused to accept P as a tenant when he got a better offer from Sears. P sued for specific performance, and D defended on the basis that the terms of the option were too indefinite to enforce and that specific performance was an inappropriate remedy.

Issue. Is specific performance available to enforce an option contract that has many uncertain terms?

Held. Yes. Judgment for P.

◆   An option contract is enforceable even when important terms are undecided, at least where it is possible to infer these material terms from the surrounding circumstances, such as D's relationship with other tenants regarding the amount of space, rental fees, etc. The contract in this case was valid.

◆   A contract may be binding yet have such substantial terms open for future negotiation that specific performance would be inappropriate. Yet an incomplete contract may be subject to specific performance in the court's discretion.

◆   The essence of specific performance is not the nature of the contract but the inadequacy of legal remedies. In this case, even if it were possible to calculate a precise measure of damages for the breach of a long-term lease contract, money damages could not compensate P for the loss of the advantages of participating in the shopping center and extending its geographic coverage.

♦ Some courts will not grant specific performance of contracts for construction of buildings because of the need for extensive supervision by the court. The better approach is to grant specific performance so long as the difficulties of supervision do not outweigh the importance of specific performance to P. In this case, there are sufficient objective bases for evaluation of the parties' contract to minimize court supervision.

---

3. **Specific Performance of Employment Contracts.**

   a. **Introduction.** Neither the employer nor the employee may specifically enforce an employment contract. The denial of affirmative relief is based on the difficulty of supervising enforcement of the decree and partly on the undesirability of imposing an employment relationship on persons who are in serious disagreement.

   b. **Injunction--**

Reier Broadcasting Co., Inc. v. Kramer, 72 P.3d 944 (Mont. 2003).

Facts. Kramer (D) was the head football coach at Montana State University (MSU). Reier Broadcasting Company, Inc. (P) had exclusive rights to broadcast MSU athletic events until the summer of 2002. In January 2001, at the behest of MSU, P contracted with D for exclusive rights to his broadcasting services until November 2004. P agreed to pay D $10,020 per year in return for D's services as an announcer and on a weekly program on MSU football, as well as providing several commercials. In the summer of 2002, MSU sought competitive bids for its broadcast rights and did not address the conflict with P's exclusive contract with D. MSU disqualified P as a potential bidder and awarded broadcast rights to Clear Channel Communications. P sought a temporary restraining order (TRO) to prevent D from providing services to Clear Channel. The court granted the TRO, but later amended it to allow D to perform media obligations in connection with his coaching job. After hearing testimony and reviewing the pleadings, the court decided that state law prohibited the issuance of an injunction under the circumstances, and the court also dissolved the TRO. P appeals.

Issue. Is a broadcasting company entitled to injunctive relief to prevent a breach of its employment contract with a college football coach for his exclusive broadcasting services?

Held. No. Judgment affirmed.

♦ Under Montana state law, an injunction cannot be granted to prevent the breach of a contract if the court cannot enforce the contract by specific performance. A personal services contract is not subject to specific enforcement.

♦ P claims the statute does not apply because P is not trying to force D to render personal services, but instead seeks to prohibit D from providing services for Clear Channel. P claims that contracts for special or unique personal services can be indirectly enforced by restraining the person from providing the services for someone else.

♦ Although the issue has never been addressed in Montana, other states' courts have held that similar state laws prevent the enforcement of negative covenants in personal services contracts. This is the best approach, because otherwise, if D were to perform at all, he would have to perform for P. This would be an indirect enforcement of the affirmative part of the contract. This does not, however, preclude P from pursuing other legal remedies.

Dissent (Cotter, J.). The TRO would prevent D from performing for any of P's competitors, but this would not amount to the indirect enforcement of the affirmative part of the contract. P is not seeking to compel D to perform. It is only seeking to prevent D from violating the non-competition provisions of his contract with P. D and MSU are seeking the court's assistance in breaching a contract they both agreed to not long ago. After having enjoyed the benefits of the contract, they should be estopped from denying the validity of the contract.

D. AGREED REMEDIES

1. **Introduction.** The parties may include in the contract specific provisions limiting or fixing the amount of damages that can be recovered in the event of a breach (*e.g.*, a liquidated damages clause).

2. **Provisions Excluding or Limiting the Amount of Damages.** The contract may provide that no damages at all may be recovered for certain types of breach (so-called "exculpatory" clauses), or that any damages recoverable be limited to a maximum sum. Courts tend to construe such provisions narrowly and will strike down provisions that are unconscionable or unreasonable.

3. **Stipulated Damages Provisions.** A contract provision may stipulate a fixed, definite sum to be paid in the event of breach (*i.e.*, "damages shall be $1,000 in the event of any breach"). The enforceability of such a provision depends on whether the court finds it to be a valid liquidated damages clause or an attempted "penalty."

a.   **Penalty provisions unenforceable.** If the court determines that the damages provision would operate as a "penalty," it is unenforceable. A provision may be held to be a penalty where it was intended as a pecuniary threat to prevent breach, or to provide a kind of security to insure the other party's performance.

b.   **Elements of enforceable provision.** If the court determines that a particular damages clause was made in good faith as an effort by the parties to estimate the actual damages that would probably arise from a breach, it may be enforced. This requires two elements:

   1)   Damages must be difficult to estimate at the time the contract was entered.

   2)   The amount agreed upon must be a reasonable forecast of actual damages; *i.e.*, a reasonable forecast of fair compensation for the harm that would occur on breach.

c.   **U.C.C.** Section 2-718 of the U.C.C. permits liquidated damages agreements if the tests above are met and if it is inconvenient or infeasible to otherwise obtain an adequate remedy; unreasonably large liquidated damages provisions are declared void as penalties.

d.   **Reasonable stipulated damages--**

Westhaven Associates, Ltd. v. C.C. of Madison, Inc., 652 N.W.2d 819 (Wis. Ct. App. 2002).

Facts. C.C. of Madison, Inc. (D) entered a 10-year lease for space in a mall owned by Westhaven Associates, Ltd. (P). Two years later, D closed its store and vacated the premises. Within four months, D stopped paying rent. P was unable to find another tenant for about a year. Under the lease, P was entitled to one of two remedies if D failed to remedy its default. First, P could terminate the lease and recover any rent due to the date of reoccupancy by P, plus liquidated damages. Second, P could choose not to terminate the lease and attempt to relet the premises and then recover from D any deficiency between the agreed lease rate and the amount for which the premises were relet, plus attorneys' fees and other expenses. P exercised the second option. D's lease rate was $49.58 per day. D did not dispute that the lease entitled P to this amount for each day between the time that it vacated and the time that the space was sublet. However, P also sought attorneys' fees of $15,670 and stipulated damages of $20 per day for the time D did not keep its premises open for business. D claimed that the attorneys' fees were not covered under the lease because they were not incurred to find a new tenant. D also claimed that the "failure to do business" provisions were unenforceable penalty provisions. The trial court found that P was entitled to its attorneys' fees but not the "failure to do business" damages. Both parties appeal.

Issues.

(i) Is P entitled to the attorneys' fees it incurred in the litigation to enforce the lease provisions against D?

(ii) Are the stipulated damages provisions in the lease reasonable and thus enforceable liquidated damages provisions?

Held. (i) No. (ii) Yes. Judgment reversed and case remanded.

♦ Under the American Rule, which Wisconsin follows, parties are generally responsible for their own attorneys' fees unless recovery is expressly allowed by contract or statute or when recovery results from third-party litigation. In this case, the lease limits recovery of attorneys' fees to those related to efforts to relet. Therefore, attorneys' fees related to suing D are not covered by the lease and should not have been awarded to P.

♦ Stipulated damages provisions are enforceable as long as they are reasonable under the totality of the circumstances. One factor is whether the parties intended the provision to provide for liquidated damages or as a penalty. D claims that the "failure to do business" provisions impose two different fees for the same conduct, so they are punitive. However, the presence of two form provisions prohibiting the same conduct does not turn the provisions into a penalty. Furthermore, the provisions, taken together, set the damages at an amount tied to D's base rent and are related to the space leased.

♦ Another factor is whether damages can be estimated at the time of contracting. When a business in a mall fails to remain open, other tenants are harmed because foot traffic is reduced. As customers shop at competitive malls and tenants lose business, the value of the mall decreases. The consequential damages to P from having one of its tenants close its business is difficult to ascertain. D did not present expert testimony that the stipulated damages provisions were unusually high compared with such provisions in similar leases at other shopping malls.

♦ A third factor is whether the stipulated damages are a reasonable forecast of the harm caused by the breach. D argues that P did not provide evidence of the mall's property value before or after D closed and thus did not establish harm. However, as the party seeking to avoid the stipulated damages provision, D had the burden of producing evidence of unreasonableness. D points out that the occupancy rate at the mall was low before it closed and actually rose after D left. But this does not mean that the breach caused P no harm. The most reasonable inference is that occupancy would have been even higher if D had remained in the mall. Indeed, another of P's tenants wrote letters relating that the closing of D's business harmed his business. D failed to meet its burden of producing evidence of unreasonableness.

NOTES

NOTES

NOTES

NOTES

NOTES

NOTES